GETTING BETTER RESULTS
FROM SPIRITUAL PRACITICE

DR. ROBERT A. RUSSELL

Audio Enlightenment Press

Giving Voice to the Wisdom of the Ages

Printed in the United States of America

First Printing, 2022
ISBN 978-1-941489-83-3

www.RobertARussell.Org

Dedication

TO CORA COSTELLO

who for eight year and more has supplied the increment in many forms, to supplant my feeble efforts, I dedicate this small tribute. Her loyalty, devotion and generosity to the cause of Truth is a rich compensation.

ROBERT A. RUSSELL

Foreword

In presenting these lessons and those contained in the two companion volumes, "Receiving What You Ask For" and "I Have Found the Way," the author does not lay claim to the discovery of any new Truth. The Truth has always been known to the few.

"There is nothing new under the sun," said Solomon. There is no new Truth. There are only varying and different ways of expressing that which has always been know. "Before Abraham and without end. Man is only the revelator of that which has always been.

Conceptions of and about Truth come to us from many sources, but it is only man's conception of them that seems to be new. Only by our understanding do we make them our own.

The author recognizes that there is probably nothing in this book which has not been said many times before. He does not claim originality to any of the Truths presented but only hopes that he may have clarified and presented it in such a way as to make a greater unfoldment possible.

What has been written here is of no importance apart from the individual consciousness or realization which makes it live. Unless the Truth grows up in us, it is to us, as though it did not exist.

Finally "all shall be taught of God."

THE AUTHOR.

Table of Contents

Dedication iii

Foreword v

Getting Better Results 1

Metaphysical Chart 5

States of Being 15

Jesus the Christ 18

Can We Know God? 21

A Definition of God 24

A True Concept of God 27

Body 30

Soul 33

Spirit 36

The Mind of the Body 39

The Mind of the Soul 42

The Mind of the Spirit 45

God Is Spirit 48

The Five Activities of Spirit 51

The Activity of Principle 54

God's Idea of Himself 57

Metaphysics 60

The Technique of Metaphysics 63

"Have Received" — The Golden Key 66

The Truth 69

Ye Shall Know the Truth 72

Applying the Truth 75

Two Classifications of Consciousness 78

On Which Plane Do You Work? 81

The Problem of Mind 84

Clearing the Mind 88

Educating the Mind 91

Formulas for Re-Educating the Subconscious Mind 94

Correlating the Mind 97

What Is Faith? 100

Putting Our Faith to Work 103

Prayer 106

Rules of Prayer 109

The Great Universal Solvent 112

By The Same Author 115

Getting Better Results

My Understanding Increases as I bless That Which I Already Have and Give Thanks for It.

"And with all thy getting get understanding." In metaphysical science, as in everything else, the Intelligence Quotient is the important thing. Good or bad results in Spiritual practice are determined by the consciousness in which one works. The Principle is always the same—true and accurate—but it always responds to the type and the grade of intelligence which uses It. The Principle is the fundamental potentiality of all things, but we can take out of It only what we have first put into It. When we have developed our intelligence sufficiently to work with God instead of against Him, we shall be able to bring about anything we desire.

The promise is, that "whatsoever ye shall ask of the Father in my name (Nature), He will give it you." Now, "whatsoever" is probably one of the biggest and most inclusive words in the Christine philosophy, because it represents everything that we can possibly conceive of as existing in God. It epitomizes the entire Kingdom of Heaven. However, for the one who reads it in the letter only, there is a catch in this word "whatsoever," because to ask the Father for "whatsoever things we desire" presupposes that we already have the Spiritual consciousness for which our asking stands. The things must be such as are in "His name" or nature; i.e., already existing in God (Good). To ask without this consciousness, Jesus says, is to "ask amiss."

There is a right and a wrong way to do everything, and in metaphysics our results will always be proportionate to our Spiritual development.

Before one can carry water from the ocean he must first have a container in which to carry it and the amount of water he carries will depend entirely upon the capacity of the container. Now let the container represent Spiritual Understanding and you will grasp the meaning of Solomon's statement, "And with all thy getting get understanding." Without understanding, we shall fail to get results.

Our greatest need therefore is not more things, more health, or more supply. We have them already, and in abundance, yeah, more than we can ever use. The great need is for Spiritual Understanding, for when we have that, we have all. We shall get better results from our practice when we are more like the Power which creates them. Results are always like their cause. Our only salvation is in a new kind of intelligence, and the sooner we make up our minds to that fact the better.

The cause of all defective states in body or circumstances is due to a poverty of intelligence or lack of understanding. We get sick because we do not know Life or because we have a wrong relationship to it. We are limited for the same reason. Jesus said, "I am come that they might have life and . . . have it more abundantly," but the Abundant Life must be interpreted in terms of spiritualized matter. Our bodies are renewed every nine months but what good is Abundant Life to us if we do not change the mold through which it manifests; if we perpetuate a limited and imperfect concept of ourselves?

"Know ye not that your body is a temple of the Holy Ghost" and that you "have power to lay it down . . . and to take it again?"

But how shall we come into possession of the Spiritual consciousness of life? Through the greater subconscious mind. "Ye shall receive power when the Holy Spirit is come upon you." The Holy Spirit comes upon us and uses us for Spiritual ends when our consciousness of God overbalances everything else in our organized existence.

"Be absent from the body and present with the Lord." If you will think of yourself as bereft of every vestige of personality, including your breath, you will find that condition of consciousness which is called the Christ and which is the necessary complement to express the Kingdom of God. "Let this mind be in you which was also in Christ Jesus." When the personal sense of sight, hearing, taste, smell and breathing have been taken away, that which is left is the Spirit and the Soul which constitute the real man. We are then in a position to claim whatsoever we will from God and "He will give it to you." We can have everything we want if we are willing to change our whole character to get it.

"Have faith in God. For verily I say unto you, That whosoever shall say unto this mountain, Be thou removed, and be thou cast into the sea; and shall not doubt in his heart (soul), but shall believe that those things which he saith shall come to pass; he shall have whatsoever he saith." "Yea, if ye have faith, though it be even as a grain of mustard seed, ye shall ask what ye will, and nothing shall be impossible unto you."

You see, it is not what we ask for with our lips (conscious minds) that God gives us, but what we ask for in our hearts (souls). "As a man thinketh in his heart so is he." Thus, when the lips (conscious mind) and heart (subconscious mind) are perfectly synchronized we can ask whatsoever we will and He will give it to us; not that He hands out something that we did not previously own, but that we become aware of that which was already ours.

"All things are yours." Do you see now why the results have been so pathetically small? Because we only asked for them with our lips. God being subjective cannot give anything to us unless we ask for it in our hearts.

"As thou hast believed (Spiritual Realization) be it done unto you." When we have a subjective realization of the things we want they shall be given to us in abundance. On the other hand, we cannot have more Life until we give up the life we have. When our consciousness of Life has been restored the results will be greater than anything we ever hope for or dreamed possible.

You will get better results in prayer, better results in practice, better results in healing when there is no longer any sense of n-e-e-d in your mind. In other words you must lift your mind above your wants before you can be conscious of the Presence of God in whom all your needs are satisfied and all your desires fulfilled.

It doesn't make any difference how great or how pressing your needs may be, when your consciousness of God overbalances your consciousness of your want, the revelation will come.

To entertain a constant sense of need is to be ungodly.

To have a consciousness of the whole is to be godly.

Metaphysical Chart

This chart, which depicts the creative process in the individual, shows man as a Trinity of Being.

The left-hand circle and all that is contained on that side of the chart represents man as personality governed by the law of alternation, where, seeing through the "glass darkly" of the human senses, "everything is necessarily apprehended as pairs of opposites in action and reaction," with all the limitations of personal self-consciousness; hence, his consciousness of Spirit and matter, health and sickness, power and weakness, knowledge and ignorance, etc., etc. It was of this state of mind that Emerson said, "Self-consciousness is the fall of man." The man who follows his senses lives in darkness. Limited and defective thought and feeling express themselves as sickness in the body and as limitation in affairs. They are held in place by the beliefs which man has accepted about himself and which were built up through the outward response of his soul. Dwelling in personality, he is governed by the law of alternation, which always leads to a state of separation and want.

Jesus counselled us to be in the world but not of it, and made it clear that it is impossible for us to attain Christ consciousness as long as we are attached to a physical or material environment. The spell of separation can be broken only as man resolutely shifts the center of his thought from matter and personality to Spirit and Truth which are the real Source of his Being. He can do this only by reforming his conception of personality and the world, and by reconstructing his consciousness of himself. He does not seek to leave the world but to mentally detach himself from it until it has "become the full expression of the Truth within him;" — until he has come to realize that Spirit is the only Reality.

Man moves from body or material consciousness into Christ or Spiritual consciousness through a new order of knowledge, or, by changing the response of his soul from sense to Spirit. By persistent effort in meditation and Silence, he gradually drops his dual consciousness for the single or Christ consciousness of perfection and wholeness which knows no opposite to and no variableness from Its own changeless and eternal nature. By following the Christ one builds a consciousness which takes no account of evil.

Turning now to the right-hand side of the chart, we find the attributes of Spirit and those divine States of Being which know no reactions to opposites and which are eternally available to man; namely, a health, power, perfection, and wealth which cannot be destroyed. These States of Being cannot be reached through thought processes or intellectual understanding, but through the conscious Recognition and subjective Realization of the Presence of God. Functioning life from the standpoint of the Divine I AM, and being of one, man can no longer accept both good and evil, but only good.

This condition of consciousness has been termed the New Dimension of Mind, to which there is no past nor future, but only the eternal NOW. "All things are NOW ready," and to dwell in this consciousness leaves nothing to be desired. This new order of consciousness will unfold to us a little at a time as we leave the old. The command of Jesus to "Leave all and follow me" means nothing more than to change the response of our souls from sense to Spirit. We have thought much about Spiritual Realities, but we shall never know them until we leave that which is unreal. To know the Truth is infinitely more important than to think it or even to believe it.

The Christ cannot appear while we are still governed by the senses. Personal self-consciousness is but partially conscious. It is still of the earth, earthy; while Christ consciousness is complete, perfect, whole and holy. It is not wanting nor lacking in anything. Disease and weakness are facts of our personality (real to it), but they are not the Truth of us. Jesus made it clear that as long as one remains in personality there is no chance of realizing the wholeness or perfection of Spirit. Thus, to follow the Christ requires a complete shift from personality to God, and we can take nothing of the old self with us, for a careful survey of personality reveals the fact that there is nothing in it which is fit to survive. That which seems good is only relatively good, and not true.

The straight line through the center of our chart represents the Principle or Divine Law of our Being. Penetrating the subjective mind of the soul, this Principle is man's power to impress upon the soul a definite word, this Principle is man's power to impress upon the soul a definite word, and, if he does not withdraw or neutralize the word with an opposite, the Divine Law will bring it into manifestation. We need to learn the law governing this Principle, for when we speak the word we are definitely setting in motion a Universal Law which must not only accept what we say, but the way in which we way it. If our treatment is given with a sense of struggle or personal effort it will manifest that way; if it is given with a sense of peace, we may look for peaceful results.

Before one can use the Principle with any degree of certainty, all sense of personal responsibility must be relinquished. All we have to do is to speak the word and Mind will carry it into certain effect, either through us or through the one for whom it is spoken. In treating either ourselves or others we always proceed in the same way, by calling our own name or that of another, and then following through the steps as outlined in the study, "Mechanics of a Treatment."

"Principle is the power that made everything: It is absolute; It will not and cannot be denied. The only thing that can deny God is yourself." If our works is done in clear consciousness and we are able to feel definitely the Presence of Spirit in our word and in the patient, there is nothing that can hinder the healing from taking place. We must continue the treatment, however, until wholeness has been restored, Jesus said, "Ye shall know the Truth," but the Truth is only as true to us as we make it through our Recognition and Realization—our awareness and consciousness of it.

The only reason we have to treat is because, through ignorance, the Principle has been misapplied; because we have "known" evil instead of "Truth," to our hurt. A better knowledge and understanding of Principle will always produce a better and more complete expression of living, or, as Jesus expressed it, a "more abundant life."

By changing the response of our souls from sense to Spirit and by keeping our minds stayed upon the Principle, we shall emerge into a full and perfect God-conscious manifestation. In Christ, the mind of the body and the mind of the Spirit are one, representing "complete self-consciousness union with Spirit" or Truth, and this Unity is "The Lamb of God which taketh away the sin of the world." Since the Principle works directly through the subconscious mind, all our work must be done in the soul. Until we learn how to live in unity with our

Principle in the soul we have no power to reveal perfection and no real knowledge of the Truth.

"Be still and know that I am" — the Principle of all things. Wholeness must come by direct impartation of the Spirit, through the soul. Thus, by dwelling in the Divine States of Being, we are living consciously in an immediate relationship with God. We are "making of the human Trinity a Divine Unity, and all states of separation are healed." When the Divine Unity Has been established, we enter the Kingdom of Heaven " as little children."

It is readily discerned that the only thing which stands between us and God is our personal self-consciousness, and when this has been swallowed up in the greater self-consciousness of Spirit we are back where we started from . . . "Before Abraham was, I AM." Then we simply let the Life, Substance, and Perfection that are innate within us, do with us as they will. In the I AM consciousness of Spirit "there shall be no more death, neither sorrow nor crying, neither shall there be any more pain; for the former things are passed away."

In pure Spirit, knowing nothing unlike Itself, there is nothing in us to get sick or die or be limited in any way. The hope of future perfection gives way to an immediate experience of perfection NOW. Definitely turning our desire inward to Spirit instead of outward to the world of things, we draw our inspiration, life and substance directly from God. The body becomes our servant and the Christ our Master.

Now, since all negative conditions are but the effects of our souls, representing ignorant ways of thinking, feeling and believing, it follows that the work of reconstruction must be done in the same place. To change an effect we must first change the cause. By refusing to allow the soul to receive suggestions from the senses ("Judge not according to appearances"), and by fixing the attention upon an opposite or Divine State of Being, we cause the subconscious mind to judge righteous judgment and to outpicture Perfection and Truth. "As a vesture shalt Thou change them, and they shall be changed."

Jesus said, "Whosoever he be of you that forsaketh not all that he hath, he cannot be my disciple." Adele M. Curtis says in her book, "The New Mysticism," that "The real death and resurrection of the body is the death and resurrection of the soul, and that is to be accomplished here and now by forsaking, denying, losing, undoing, and letting go the imperfect self-consciousness which we built up as the result of our evolutionary experience, and building in its place a new and perfect consciousness of ourselves as we are," in Spirit and in Truth. The new consciousness has to be formed in the soul before we can be conscious of it in our objective experience.

The outer circle of the chart, enfolding and intersphering all the others, represents the one Mind in which we all live, move and have our being. It is represented as a circle because a circle is the only picture we can draw of God and because it is the only symbol which can be expanded in all directions ad infinitum and without any break in its continuity.

Actually, there is no such thing as your mind and my mind or anybody else's mind; there is only God's mind in which we all live, move and have our being. In reality, the mind of the body, the mind of the soul and the mind of the Spirit are just so many uses of the one Mind. They are the causes of our physical effects.

All things are related to Mind as ideas, and for that reason we do not seek to demonstrate things, but to embody ideas. Mind is the medium through which everything comes to us as the result of an idea or word held, and released, in the mind. As we hold the word in mind through the power of the will until it is fully formed and then let it fall into the soul through the power realization, it comes back to us in form. As the Spirit (conscious mind) impregnates the soul with an idea, the Spirit produces the form on the experience plane. Acting upon the substance of God which fills all space, the Spiritual child is born.

As Ernest Holmes says: "There is one first cause, having three aspects: Spirit, Soul, and Body; i.e., Cause, Medium and Effect; the Father, Son and Holy Ghost; Masculine activity, Feminine activity, and the Result" — which have the same meaning as the triad of Recognition, Realization, and Revelation.

The V-shaped canal descending through the center of the chart and continuing through the Experience Plane, represents the Will and is merely a vise to hold the word on its course toward the region of Spirit which is the realm of all Power and Action. In this realm the word takes form and comes back to us as a Reality — a manifestation of Spirit — on the objective plane. As we let fall the words or images of our thought into the soul, they are acted upon by the Spirit and come back to us as the embodiment or form of the word which has been spoken.

In the center of this opening is a small black bar which is designated as the "trap door." This door is opened quickly by the power of Spiritual Realization, bringing the consciousness of God and the consciousness of man together in perfect Unity. If this door is open our words "accomplish that where unto they are sent." If it is not open, our words become "clouds without rain." It is obvious, therefore, that before our prayer can be answered the trap door must be open. Jesus said, "It is done unto you according to your faith" or belief. That is, there must be a perfect correlation between the conscious and subconscious minds. If the soul does not receive the word which is spoken then the Spirit has no medium through which to express. When the door is open then you can "ask whatsoever ye will and it shall be done unto you."

Jesus gave us the key to open this door in the following words, "Leave all and follow me;" "He that loseth his life shall find it;" which have the same meaning as Paul's words, "Be absent from the body and present with the Lord;" and "Dying to self." When we are absent from self-consciousness according to personality (which means everything contained on the left-hand side of the chart) then we are in a right relationship to God. We are in a position to receive from Him whatsoever we ask. It is then that "ye shall see the heavens open, and the angels (Spiritual thoughts) of God ascending and descending upon the son of man."

Jesus said, "The Father that dwelleth in me, He doeth the works," but God does not do the works until we are out of our thought or until we recognize Him as the only power in our lives. In order to help another individual therefore, his "trap door," too, must be open as well as our own. Both minds must be perfectly oriented to the Mind and Will of God. Otherwise he cannot receive the benefits of our treatment.

How do we know that there is a "trap door" in mind? Because if it were not for this safety valve every thought, good, bad or indifferent, would be instantly manifested. If we thought we were going to be sick we would get sick immediately. If we thought we were going to die we should die. The subconscious mind being entirely obedient to the conscious mind and having no power of choice, would be helpless to avert the greater disasters of our erroneous and ignorant ways of thinking. It is fortunate for us, therefore, that our occasional and vagrant thoughts do not objectify themselves immediately in our experience. There is always the time element of the trap door between the objective outpicturing of our subjective states and it is because of this that we have the opportunity of correcting our imperfect beliefs, thoughts and feelings and substituting the Word of Truth. Thinking after the manner of Jesus' appointing we nullify and reverse the results that would otherwise manifest in the circumstances and conditions of our life. We may think of it then as that element of mind which keeps law and order in our lives, and until we learn how to use the mind for constructive purposes only, it is well that this "trap door" should remain closed, for when it is closed only our habitual states of mind have any influence in our lives.

Recognition is the masculine function of Mind (intellect) conveying the word of Truth to the "trap door" where it is held in place by the Will until the consciousness of the word has been formed in us.

Realization is the power or feeling of the Whole Mind which meets the word at the "trap door," opens the door, and brings the word into the soul for gestation.

Revelation is the "Word made flesh" through the power of the Spirit by which the word is united with Universal Substance and given back to us in form to "dwell among us."

The Spirit is the Mind which recognizes the Will and uses it for constructive purposes only.

The subconscious mind is not responsible for the imperfect conditions which she has built into our lives, because being subjective she builds according to the suggestions, thoughts, words and feelings received from the intellect or conscious mind. To build perfect conditions we must change our ways of judging, thinking and feeling. It should be noted by every student that the only purpose and function of the Will is to hold the word in place and to still the senses while the Spiritual Word is being born. Any other use of the Will is destructive. The Will is never creative but always directive.

The plane of experience represents the conditions of Life, which is but the mirror or effect of the soul. Whatever use is made of Principle is expressed on the experience plane. We can remake the experience plane by changing the habits of the soul, for the use we make of Principle becomes the law or experience of our Life.

Within the Principle is man's key to every situation, but salvation must come to him ultimately through his realization of the whole, through his perfect unity with God. As man thinks within himself, he thinks upon God's Mind and sets in motion the law which reveals the perfection or substance that was already there. Since there is but one Mind we may consciously recognize and realize the Truth for ourselves or others and cause the law to work for us as we direct. Man never creates: he simply uses Divine Law to reveal the States of Being which fill all space and are only hidden from us because of our failure to recognize that they are, and always have been.

Personality is a persistent, relentless struggle between ease and want, between achievement and despair, and between health and sickness. Spirit and Its inevitable Reality is that which is, and ought to be. We must release the "imprisoned splendour" and let it come forth.

States of Being

Be still and know that I am God

Be still and know that I am Spirit

Be still and know that I am Life

Be still and know that I am Love

Be still and know that I am Power

Be still and know that I am Unity

Be still and know that I am Truth

Be still and know that I am Holiness

Be still and know that I am Faith

Be still and know that I am Joy

Be still and know that I am Peace

Be still and know that I am Knowledge

Be still and know that I am Principle

Be still and know that I am Freedom

Be still and know that I am Beauty

Be still and know that I am Understanding

Be still and know that I am Grace

Be still and know that I am Goodness

Be still and know that I am Wisdom

Be still and know that I am Righteousness

Be still and know that I am Right Action

Be still and know that I am Substance.

Before one can eliminate anxiety, as Jesus counselled, he must use words in his treatments which have no association with personalities, objects, or things on the relative plane. Before one can develop Spiritual consciousness "without variance," he must use language which does not arouse in him contradictory thoughts of matter as opposed to Spirit. Before our word can be absolute, our consciousness must be of one kind, that is without alternation or reaction to opposites.

In the highest Truth we can only associate ourselves with words which convey Spiritual ideas. "Spiritual consciousness is the consciousness of Spirit," — (clear consciousness). "And my God shall supply all your needs according to His riches in Christ Jesus," — Christ Jesus representing Spiritual consciousness (without variation) which is the realization of all things and at the same time the realization of no thing. "If ye be risen with Christ seek those things which are above" the realm of the things.

"Every good and every perfect gift cometh down from above" — the realm of Spiritual ideas. "Beloved, I wish above all things that thou mayest prosper and be in health." True prosperity and health come out of one's consciousness of the whole. "Spirit being Infinite, transcends the realm of things," for if Spirit were any thing or confined to any thing it would immediately lose its essential nature or Infinity. "Seek ye first the Kingdom of God (Realization of Spirit) and all . . . things shall be added unto you."

The word "metaphysics" means literally, above forms or above things. In the truest sense it is an abstract science, and unless one is working on the abstract basis (above the realm of the concrete) he is not following Jesus who said, "Leave all and follow me." Practically all our instructions in the past have been an attempt to realize things, which is equivalent to working in reverse. When Jesus said, "Know no man after the flesh"

"Call no man on earth your Father" — "He that loseth his life shall find it" — and "Judge not according to appearances," — He was urging upon man the necessity of entering that realm of consciousness which can only be described as "without form and void."

"Leave all" on the relative plane, does not mean to give up our business, possessions, homes and friends, but to clear our consciousness of them. As we follow Him we shall refine our conception of things and have a new relationship to them. "If ye abide in me (clear consciousness) and my words (States of Being) abide in you (understanding of Spirit), then ask whatsoever ye will and it shall be done unto you." There is no human need that cannot be met by one or other of the States of Being mentioned above.

That I may know the Spirit within me.

Jesus the Christ

"Out of Zion, the Perfection of Beauty, God Hath Shined Forth" —
In Christ.

"Behold, a virgin shall conceive, and bear a son, and shall call
His name Emmanuel" (God with us)

There is a distinction between Jesus and Christ, and yet there
is no distinction because the two are one. Jesus is the name
given to the man who most fully and perfectly demonstrated
the Christ. "Of the increase of His government there shall
be no end." The Christ in Jesus was the embodiment of all
Law, government, Spiritual understanding, wisdom and
knowledge of God.

The first sentence of His first sermon was, "Blessed are the
poor in Spirit, for there's is the Kingdom of Heaven." And
again "Blessed are they which do hunger and thirst after
righteousness for they shall be filled." Jesus made it clear that
the blessings of Heaven were for those who understood God
and made a right use of Divine Law. Righteousness means
right use of Spiritual law.

Jesus was the Son of man. Christ is the Son of God. Jesus, the
Christ, symbolizes perfected humanity, or the Truth revealed.
Jesus was the type man using the Spiritual power which is
possessed by, and indigenous in all men; waiting to be
recognized by them. To embody the Christ one must embody
the same Truth and understanding He had.

"I and the Father are one." Christ is the very essence of Life,
Substance, and Power within every man. "Christ is all." He is

our point of contact with God. "All things are delivered unto me" — the Christ. "All things that the Father hath are mind" — the Christ's. Thus, to have Christ is to have all. To have "Christ in you" is to be in Heaven. To have "Christ in you" is to have Life in you which knows no death; health in you which knows no weakness; peace in you which knows no confusion.

Christ Is the Way. "No man cometh unto the Father but by me."

Christ Is the Truth. "I am the Truth." "thy word is Truth." "The Truth shall make you free." How are we to know the Truth? Except ye become converted (turned around) and become as little children, ye shall in no wise enter the Kingdom of Heaven."

Christ Is Spirit Life. "This is life eternal, that they might know Thee, — the only true God, and Jesus Christ, — whom Thou hast sent."

Christ Is God's Consciousness of Himself. "Whosoever believeth that Jesus is the Christ, is born of God."

Christ Is the Son of God. "As many as are led by the Spirit (Christ) of God, they are the Sons of God."

Christ Is Power. "Ye shall receive power after the Holy Ghost is come upon you." Why can we do the words that Jesus did? Because we are "joint heirs with Christ." And whatsoever ye shall ask in my name (Christ consciousness), that will I do, that the Father may be glorified in the Son." "If ye abide in me (Christ consciousness) and my words (heavenly language) abide in you, ye shall ask what ye will and it shall be done unto you." "The Father loveth the Son (Christ) and hath given all things into His hand."

By what authority do we proclaim the Kingdom of Heaven on earth, the healing of the body, the redemption of man, and the supremacy of Spirit over human thought? "For this purpose the Son of God (Christ) was manifested, that He might destroy the works of the devil (divided mind)."

"Ye are Christ's; and Christ is God's"
I "stand fast in the liberty wherewith Christ hath made me free."

Can We Know God?

The conscious recognition of the presence of God is the fulfillment of every right desire.

Unless our idea of God is true it is not demonstrable. The great question asked by humanity for countless ages is, "Can we know God?" That there is a God we have accepted on faith, but we must have proof, irrefutable proof, that God is and that He is accessible to us. It is the task of the next six lessons, therefore, to define what we mean by God and to prove His accessibility, helpfulness, and response to the individual mind.

Men have spent much time and energy collecting facts which they believed would eventually carry them to the heights and freedom, but have found them impotent. They are now coming to a realization that God consciousness is not built alone on human knowledge or the facts they so laboriously father, but that it is a state of mind engendered by the processes of meditation, contemplation and silence, in which the material instincts, grown to great proportion in the struggle for existence, are controlled by one's consciousness of the whole and that life at its best eventually becomes an exemplification of cooperation with that which we know to be true. As yet we have taken but a few steps from paganism. Men were not long in discovering that knowledge is always potential power, but they have still to understand that only its wise use is liberty.

Of all the empires of the world that men have made an effort to control, the one they know most about and have done the least with is the one within themselves. To bring it under control is to grew up—become mature—to fit our abilities to mold the outer world to our uses and to harmonize the relationship between ourselves and our environment. We have no choice in this matter; we make these adjustments either of our own free will or against it, but make them we do. Life has a way of educating us whether we like it or not.

Schools of metaphysics give us the frame work upon which to hang the intangible fabric of Spiritual consciousness, but the consciousness Itself, the understanding that is possible only through Recognition, Realization, and the training of every faculty, comes only from within. It has as its ultimate objective the realization that we are each a part of a great and homogeneous whole that has had no beginning in time, and by the

same token can have no ending; that matter and Spirit are but different manifestations of the same changeless Substance; and that only as we permit our souls to carry us away from self, the mistaken sense of here and now, can we escape the slavery that makes us such close kin to the brute.

Without God consciousness we can neither see straight, feel right, think truly, nor advance with reasonable economy of effort. Progress in Spiritual work, therefore, is a sustained movement toward something better than what the present can offer. If that progress is to become more than a mere word, it must be given meaning through cooperation with Principle and a direct experience of God.

Can we know God? I may answer for myself alone when I say that I can do. My knowledge of Him is entirely immediate and intuitive. I have a "feeling" of dependence upon Him together with a "feeling" of confidence in Him that serves to relieve me from many burdensome cares. I know that I can commune with Him and I know that I receive from Him according to my belief. For me He does exist as a Presence with whom I commune. My knowledge is entirely immediate, having no intermediary, — based upon intuition and feeling.

I shall dwell in a "peaceful habitation," a "sure dwelling" and in a "quiet resting place."

A Definition of God

To "Know the Truth" means to have the true idea
of Principle or God.

Principle is Life: There is no better life than the one we have now, because Life, no matter where we find It, will be none other than our consciousness of It. "God is Life" — the "unmixed, unvarying goodness which knows no opposite." Life is that which lives, and power is the energy by which it operates. Life is that quality of perfection running through all, which enables anything to be what it is. We conclude therefore, that Principle is first Life. It must live before it can do anything else.

"In the beginning God" — Life. Could there be any existence before Life? Could there be anything before consciousness? If God existed before His consciousness (life) then there must have been a time when He was lifeless or dead. Obviously there cannot be consciousness without life, and there cannot be mind without consciousness, therefore Life and consciousness must be the very same thing — God. "I am Alpha and Omega." At both ends of our existence is life, therefore life is without end. "God is not the God of the dead, but of the living, for all live unto Him." "I am the living One." "I (Principle) am come that they might have life and have it more abundantly."

There is no life nor world to come. The only life we shall have is the one that is now Present with us. The life more abundant spoken of by Jesus is the consciousness of true or "Spirit Life" within ourselves. "For until we have that life which was also in Christ Jesus we are only half alive."

Principle is Love: That which loves, gives. God expresses Himself by giving Himself to us. God as love expresses Himself in terms of creation. "Love is the fulfilling of the Law." It is the power that attracts and binds all creation together in a divine pattern. Love is the harmonious working of all its parts. Principle therefore is as much She as He, and as much It as She or He.

Principle is Mind: "In Him we live, and move, and have our being." Mind is the Intelligence and Law by which God governs what he creates. Life must become conscious of Itself; before it can express Truth and use Law It must be able to think. Before It can love It must first live. "There is but one Mind common to all men." "Let this mind be in you which was also in Christ Jesus." The mind of Christ is the true consciousness of God, the Spiritual understanding of life which is eternal, indivisible, indestructible, unvarying, changeless, and which "knows no possibility of reaction or alternation from Itself." It only awaits the understanding, and the "cooperation of our intelligence to manifest Itself in us here and now as the Spiritual consciousness of the Christ or ultimate man."

Principle is Spirit: Spirit is that part of man which enables him to be conscious of himself. Spirit is that which he really is. "The Spirit is the power that knows Itself in us." God must always know Himself; therefore Spirit is self-conscious Life. It is the inner meaning of the I AM. "'Tis the Spirit that quickeneth, the flesh profiteth nothing."

Principle is Truth: The Spirit that knows Itself must be true to Itself. Truth is the Law by which God proves Himself. "If ye abide in me." Truth must be law abiding. Truth is that which conforms to God. It is the true idea of God, and when we are conscious of It within ourselves we lose all sense of limitation, separation and evil.

My security lies in my essential unity with God.

Realizing that I am the Presence of Principle, I bring the Law of God — Good — into operation in my life, and live abundantly.

A True Concept of God

"The Sculptor Turns From The Marble To His Model In Order To Perfect His Conception."

The Mosaic conception of God was that of a King, Creator and Judge. The Christian conception is that of a Father, Savior, and Comforter. The metaphysical or Spiritual conception is that of Principle or Law, which according to the Founder of our religion is the correct understanding of Divine Being. Jesus Christ taught that God is Infinite Spirit, Life, Mind, Truth, Love, Intelligence, Law and Principle, and that man embodies these heavenly qualities within himself. To abide in (relate ourselves to) these qualities is to have in us that same mind which was also in Christ Jesus.

The Master declared these facts from the beginning of His ministry, but His hearers, lacking Spiritual understanding, interpreted Deity in the familiar terms of personality. When Jesus spake of God as Father they thought of Him as a glorified man or Infinite Personality, which gave rise to our anthropomorphic concept of a man God. Hence, the "strife of opposites" and the many sided consciousness which constitutes our knowledge of Spirit.

The one thing which the whole world needs today more than anything else is a new consciousness, and a more intelligent understanding of God. "I, if I be lifted up, will draw all men (manifestation) unto me." As we rise in consciousness above the old ideas of personality to the Spiritual conception of God as Principle we shall find that we are not only able to receive God, but to prove Him in all our affairs of mind, body

27

and estate. The true understanding of God is the answer to every problem. "Behold, I make all things new." The new conception of God as Principle involves a new relationship to Life, a new relationship to health, a new relationship to supply; a greater understanding of Jesus, of the world and of time. As man discovers and specializes these powers through his own mind, there is nothing in his world that will remain untouched or unchanged. By declaration and realization of the Spiritual facts of Being, he will lift his thought into the realm which is perfection and express that perfection in his life.

"The Father is the Intelligence or Understanding within man that reveals to him his perfect identity. After man fully understands this, he is then the Son knowing the Father. To know both God and man as Jesus knew them, individual man must train himself to think with the divine consciousness, the same mind that was in Jesus. This state of thought always operates as righteous judgment."[1]

To understand Divine Principle is to understand that "all things are yours." There is absolutely nothing we cannot have if we ask of Principle in terms of Itself and not, as has been our custom in the past, in terms of objects and things. To ask Principle in "terms of Itself" would be to "have that mind (God consciousness) in us which was also in Christ Jesus." The divine order in revealing the Truth is, first, to understand God, and then, to act upon our understanding. "Prove me now herewith saith the Lord."

God is Principle — "The Intelligent Power back of and through everything; the Unconditioned which nothing can limit; that

---

[1] From "The Stranger Within" — Fred E. Dobbins.

from which everything comes; the self-knowing Mind back of everything; the Heavenly Father and Eternal Mother of all; the one and only conscious Mind in the Universe, personal to all who believe in Him. And the only way we can conceive of the Divine Being is through our own nature, for His Spirit is our Spirit."[2]

Father, let that "mind be in me which was also in Christ Jesus." "Let there be," and it was so.

---

2 From "Science of Mind" — Ernest Holmes.

Body

"But We All, With Unveiled Face Beholding As In a Mirror The Glory of The Lord, Are Transformed Into The Same Image From Glory To Glory . . ."

Jesus' statement that "Flesh and blood cannot inherit the Kingdom of heaven" refers not to man's body, but to his false sense of life and to his wrong concept of the body. These two, constituting man's consciousness, have the same meaning as St. Paul's designation of personality as the "carnal mind" — "For the mind of the flesh is death; but the mind of the Spirit is life and peace: because the mind of the flesh is enmity against God; for it is not subject to the law of God, neither indeed can it be; and they that are in the flesh cannot please God."

It is not man's body that is subject to disease and death, but his erroneous ideas of his body. If one views the body from the standpoint of personality or appearance he will think of it as a solid, material form. If he views it from the Spiritual perspective he will see it as a changing, flowing, formless, substance which is forever coming and going. The billions of cells composing the body are in a continuous state of flow. They are like a river, forever flowing; the Spirit alone maintains the identity.

The outer body changes so rapidly that we do not actually get up in the morning with the same body we took to bed the night before. The onward march from infancy to childhood, from childhood to youth, from youth to adolescence, from adolescence to maturity, is nothing more than man's passage from one body to another. The body of the adult has changed many times during its earthly existence, and yet through the innumerable changes there is a continuity of feeling and identity which does not change. The body at forty contains not a single cell which it had at twenty, and yet man is conscious of being the same individual he was in the first body he ever had.

What does this prove other than that the body which we thought of as solid matter and which the X-ray has shown to be transparent, is nothing more than an aggregation of infinitely small particles arranged in such order as to produce definite forms — the forms being determined by something which is not material, but mental or Spiritual?

There is but one Substance from which all forms are made, and which is fluidic and subjective to our thought. The body we have today shall be changed tomorrow. Spinoza said, "Substance is plastic and Spirit is compelling," and this theory has been held by all the great philosophers of all time. Our bodies therefore, are but an extension of our minds — they are the objectification or externalization of our thought.

What a man is or what a man has in the outer world is the sum total of his feeling and thought about himself and his affairs. Everything he has in form is directly related to the body of his thought. The personality is one with all matter in the material world. The state of man's body or his business represents his consciousness of them. The so-called physical body is but a manifestation of man's mind in form. It is what he "believes" about himself.

But since the substance of man's body is plastic to his thought it is subject to change and improvement. The question is often asked, "Why, if man is made in the image of Perfection does

31

he manifest a defective body?" And, "Why if the substance of his body is renewed from day to day does he not express perfect health?" Because he does not "know the Truth," and because today he continues to provide the same mold or mental pattern he provided yesterday. The remedy is found in Paul's words: "Be not fashioned according to this world." When man understands that his body is but the effect or extension of his soul he will change it into a more perfect form by reconstructing his ways of thinking and feeling about it. "Flesh and blood" is but a way of thinking and feeling.

> *My material body is not true;*
> *The Christ body is the Truth.*

Soul

The Soul answers never in words, but by the thing itself
that is inquired after — Emerson.
The Soul is the perceiver and revealer of Truth — Emerson

The Metaphysical Bible Dictionary defines "soul" as "man's consciousness — that which he has apprehended or developed out of Spirit; also the impressions which he has received from the outer world . . . Body is the form of expression of both Spirit and soul. The body is the outer court of the soul, and an exact representative, in form, of the ideals that are revolving in the inner realms of its domain . . . The soul touches both the inner realm of Spirit, from which it receives direct inspiration, and the external world, from which it receives impressions."

Man is a soul and not a body. The soul is the affirmative factor in all his experience. It is the storehouse of all his memories, experiences, beliefs and emotions. It is the seat of both understanding and misunderstanding and the great creative and feeling center of realization. Man's body and affairs are always under the absolute dominion of his soul, causing health and wealth or sickness and poverty. It is through the soul that we accept or reject the Truth. It is through the soul that we identify ourselves with good or evil, power or weakness, perfection or imperfection, but being impersonal it neither cares nor knows what we use it for.

The scriptural name for soul is "heart." It has also been called "The Holy Ghost," "the womb of nature" and the "Holy Mother." Being receptive and responsive to Spirit (conscious thought) and giving birth to the ideas or cognitions of the conscious mind, the soul is feminine in its nature. As we impress divine ideas upon the soul through the power of Recognition (conscious thought) and Realization (subjective feeling), the Revelation that comes back to us is "The Word made flesh." "Things which are seen are not made of things which do appear."

Matter is simply the immaterial and invisible substance of the soul which is formed by the power of our word — Recognition and Realization. The soul being neutral receives all our ideas and gives them form in the outer world. It has no choice and knows neither good nor bad. It knows only to do do. Things, therefore, are extensions or objectifications of the soul and Spirit working through Self-realization. Soul always says "Yes." It never says "No." It is always receptive, passive, plastic and impersonal. It is the medium of Recognition, Realization and Revelation, or the thought, the power, and the expressing.

The body of man and the body of his affairs are but the results of his "knowing," working through soul or law. The cause of everything in the outer world of effects is in the soul. The body is the form of our feeling of ourselves. It will always express the quality of consciousness or feeling of the soul. If the soul is sick the body will be sick. If the soul feels poor the man will express conditions of limitation. We must gain control over our bodies and circumstances by gaining control over our souls. All dominion begins within the soul.

"Flesh and blood," we said in a previous study, "cannot inherit the Kingdom of God," but there is nothing to prevent us from changing our ignorant idea of matter and bringing it into its right relationship to Spirit. The soul will believe anything we wish to believe and it will express that belief in outward form.

It is a sad commentary upon our intelligence that we get sick. We do not know God, whom to know aright is eternal health. When we possess our souls we shall possess our bodies. The soul will make any kind of a body we choose to have, but the quality of the body will always depend upon the quality of the soul — the habit of its belief. When we understand matter as consciousness we shall express perfection and health.

"Build thee more stately mansions, O my soul."

Spirit

"Be Still And Know That I AM Spirit;
In Me There Is No Matter."

"The Spirit is the divine center in man and is always in the absolute; it does not become involved in effects, but stands as the creative cause of the absolute good." — The Metaphysical Bible Dictionary.

"The Spirit is the power that knows Itself." Being Infinite Mind or consciousness, the only consciousness It could have would be Self-consciousness, that is, conscious of nothing but Itself and conscious of nothing outside Itself. Spirit is first Cause or God. It is also that part of man which enables him to be self-conscious — either self-conscious in personality or Self-conscious in God. "There is a Spirit in man." But whether Universal or personal, mind always functions Life from the basis of the personal pronoun. "I."

Spirit has also been defined as the Universal I AM, which is an absolute statement of the all-inclusiveness and absolute essence of God. Whether in man or in God, Spirit is Conscious Mind and functions Life in relation to every other form from the basis of the pronoun "I" or self-consciousness. The realm of self-consciousness is the realm of ideas, and ideas are the means by which consciousness becomes self-conscious. As an illustration, a man's consciousness of his body is made up of his ideas concerning it. If he believes that his life is dependent upon his body, he will be anxious for its life. "Is not life more than raiment?"

When we know Life as Jesus knew it then we shall have less concern for the body. We shall see the utter impossibility of taking the body away from the Presence of Life. Man must outgrow his personal sense of life or perish. It is not Life that changes, but man's idea about it. Spirit is complete, perfect and whole, knowing only the eternal NOW. 'Man's Spirit is the Kingdome of God," but he has not yet come into possession of himself: "he has only got as far as the soul." "There is a Spirit in man," and when the soul knows the Spirit as she now knows the body she will have Life in herself. The body, soul and Spirit will become one.

If the conscious mind receives its suggestions and impressions from the outer world it cannot receive its perfection of Truth. Until it can cease to identify itself with its old ideas and feelings which it has acquired through ignorance, it cannot express newness of life. All our imperfections have been made through ignorance and we must remake them through our conscious recognition and realization of the Truth. We shape them in our conscious thought and give them form through the subjective mind of the soul. But what a man has made he can unmake by the unfoldment and realization of new ideas. "Behold I (Spirit) make all things new." The Spirit is always expressed. That which is involved must evolve.

Spirit passes into form through the Trinity of creation—Recognition, Realization, and Revelation. Man does not create, but his consciousness of Spirit makes his word creative. Spirit makes our thoughts and words live. Man simply uses substance through the activity and law of his own mind. His conscious thought, acting upon the soul, produces a revelation. Recognition is the play of Life upon Itself through self-realization. As man's conscious thought lets fall its ideas into the soul, they are acted upon through the power of his

37

realization and pass into form. Involved within the idea is everything necessary to unfold and express the idea in form.

When we identify ourselves with Spirit (Divine Mind) then it is quite impossible for us to believe in any other mind. The human and Divine have never been two men but two ideas or concepts of the same man. The two states are simply two different ways of looking at ourselves.

Returning to the Father's House (consciousness) we discover that Spirit is one not two.

Spirit becomes active in me by my conscious recognition of the Presence of God.

The Mind of the Body

"Our Problem Is To Arouse Sufficient Power To Lift Up The Whole Consciousness Until We See With An Understanding Heart."

The mind of the body is the objective mind, finite mind, the mind of the flesh, the carnal mind, the natural mind, the intellect, the self-choosing mind, the willful mind, the personal mind, the mind of self-determination, of volition and will.

Actually, there is but One Mind with three distinct phases of activity which are called conscious, subconscious and superconscious—the mind of the body, the mind of the soul and the mind of the Spirit; and the three are One. They are One because a careful analysis of the three reveals he fact they they act and interact upon each other.

The objective mind, which is also called conscious mind, is that phase of mental activity which relates man to the outer world of appearance, to his personality, and to his environment. This phase of mind has also been called the "sense" mind and has been referred to in the Bible as "through a glass darkly." Being governed by the law of alternation, this mind necessarily apprehends everything in pairs of opposites; good and evil life and death, health and sickness, wealth and poverty, etc., etc. The personal mind being dual in its nature has accepted both extremes which explains our illusion of separation.

The objective mind is man's erroneous conception of himself. It is also his Spiritual Self unrealized. It is what he knows about himself. It is also his power to unknown. The fleshly minded man cannot deny that he is imperfect as he knows himself in the personality (fleshly mind). Judging by appearances his consciousness is lacking in completeness and wholeness.

The objective mind, unrelated to Spirit, is but partially conscious of itself; knowing only the personality or outward and physical form it is limited in its expression. "Sin, therefore, is a fact of our personality but it is not the Truth of us." The Truth is that God and man are one, but until we have unified ourselves with this Truth—recognize that Spirit is the only power in our lives—we cannot be free from the separate self. Only as we bring the body and soul together can we realize the Spirit of Unity. "God and man are forever one, but God is never man, and is never God."

Self-consciousness, divorced from Spirit, is chiefly personal and objective. It must be redeemed by our expansion into the full and perfect consciousness of Christ through an habitual and positive response to the good.

In Spirit—Realization of one Presence and Power—man is perfect and whole. The contradiction is in the objective mind (which is God's Mind unrealized), between appearance and reality, between what we know about ourselves and what Spirit knows about us. "So then with the Mind (Spirit) I myself serve the law of God; but with the flesh the law of sin." "For to be carnally minded is death; but to be spiritually minded is life and peace." It was of the objective mind that St. Paul said, "Be ye transformed by the renewing of your mind," and of the Spirit that he said, "Be perfectly joined together in the same mind and in the same judgment," which is the right use or relationship to the only mind we have—using it in the right way, so to speak.

The purpose of metaphysical science is to teach man how to live consciously in immediate and personal relationship with Spirit, always aware of Its Presence with him. Before we can instruct the subconscious mind through which the law works, we must reconstruct our ways of thinking. If we have used the Principle destructively we must now learn to use it constructively.

We shall always attract to us those things which are like our thought or the consciousness in which we work. The objective man is the body and personality. The objective mind is man's consciousness of himself. Conscious mind is the mind you are using right now. It is the Spirit of you because it is the medium through which you reach the subconscious mind and is the instrument through which you discover Spirit.

The only mind we ever use is the Mind of God. Our mind will become divine when we use it in the right way. When we use it constructively we get good results; when we use it destructively we get evil results. The mind of the body is the mind that must be renewed (rightly related to Spirit) before we can enter the Kingdome of Heaven.

The secret of having all our needs supplied is to bring our human mind and will into subjection to the Divine Mind and Will. Job recognized the necessity of this surrender when he said, "I know that Thou canst do everything and that no thought can be with-holden from Thee." That was Job's acknowledgment of the supremacy of Spirit and we read of him that "the Lord gave Job twice as much as he had before." When we put ourselves and our affairs completely in God's hands then the Truth will be demonstrated in our lives. Let us remember however that we cannot employ Divine Law with the unnatural processes of the human mind.

Jesus Christ is now here, raising me to His consciousness of divine understanding, and all my mental activities are spiritual."

41

The Mind of the Soul

"God-Mind Is, Under The Law Of Thought, Constantly Seeking To Release Its Perfection In You."

The psychologist tells us that "all mental states are followed by bodily activity of some sort . . . all states of mind, even mere thoughts and feelings, are motor in their consequences." — (James.) The tendency of every thought is to express itself as an effect. The quotation above means that our habitual conscious states of mind become subconscious states, and that subconscious states become conscious or objective states. In other words, the personality reproduces all the beliefs of the soul.

The subconscious mind is the mind of the soul. The subconscious mind receives impressions from the conscious mind and acts upon them. It is also the place where our thoughts, mental pictures and impressions go and eventually return to us as memory. The dictionary defines "subjective" as "the impression which an object makes on the mind." The idea or concept is the impression which the mind receives.

The Spirit is conscious mind: the soul is subconscious mind and our consciousness of God is Superconscious Mind. The conscious mind is the knower; the subconscious mind is the receiver and actor, the doer and executor. "Every object comes into consciousness in a two-fold way as simply thought of, i.e., as perceived or conceived, and as admitted or denied, i.e., as believed or disbelieved."

The Trinity of mind is Recognition, Realization, and Revelation; word, Law and effect; Spirit, Soul and Body;

42

thought, feeling and action; Father, Son and Holy Ghost; Life, Mind and form. The subconscious mind is always obedient to the conscious mind and "man, by thinking, can bring into his experience whatsoever he desires, if he thinks correctly and becomes a living embodiment of his thoughts. This is not done by holding thoughts, but by knowing the Truth."

The rule to remember is that everything that goes into the subconscious mind must come out of it as an experience. The personality is but the sum total of man's subconscious beliefs. It permeates every atom of his being through and through. The expression of the subconscious mind can be changed only through deep feeling or realization of the Truth. If one would change to a higher order or consciousness he merely changes his habits of response. Instead of receiving his knowledge from the outer world of appearance he turns within to Reality or Truth.

The subconscious mind is at work constantly, carrying on all the involuntary functions of he body—digestion, glandular secretion, assimilation, circulation, respiration; and serves to repair the wear and tear of the conscious thinking. It does all this without the conscious thinking. It does all this without the conscious thought or will of man. It knows how to transmute the various elements of food into flesh and blood so as to maintain perfect health in the body. It has unlimited power for acquiring all the blessings of life and of keeping the body in a perfect state of health.

If we could trust our whole lives to the Spirit working through the subconscious mind just as we trust the mechanism of our bodies to it there is nothing we could not do or accomplish. Drawing its inspiration from God it has all the wisdom of all the ages past. It is always willing and competent to give us anything we desire provided we are rightly related to what we are seeking. Being always obedient to the conscious thought and will of man, it can be trained to do anything.

Our work is not to change the action of the subconscious mind, but to bring it into a right relationship with God. If it is at present perpetuating disagreeable characteristics, traits, heredities and beliefs, we change these manifestations by the refinement of our conceptions. It is natural for the subconscious mind to express Perfection. It is unnatural for it to express imperfection. Defects in consciousness are but the result of imperfect subconscious training. A man can change his heredity only as he changes his subconscious beliefs. This is done by knowing the Truth that "I and my Father are one."

Remember that it is the mental antecedent of your problem that you have to deal with and not the effect. It is quite impossible to treat unpleasant facts or conditions out of existence so long as we still nurture the consciousness or mental state which caused it. Defective conditions can be annihilated only as we remove the beliefs that sustain them. They can be displaced only by a greater realization of the Truth. When the Truth becomes motor (habitual in its response it will not only remove all support from evil but will do away with the demonstration of evil. Our freedom therefore is dependent upon our ability to build up something in consciousness which is big enough to displace the negative thoughts or demonstrations which have been holding us in bondage. Renewing the mind is a scientific procedure. When the subconscious work is properly done the objective manifestation must conform.

"Let the words of my mouth and the meditation of my heart be acceptable in Thy sight, O Lord, my strength and my redeemer."

The Mind of the Spirit

"Blessed Is He That Hath Part In The First Resurrection: . . .
They Shall Be Priests Of God And Of Christ."

The divine order in revealing the Truth is from the conscious mind to the subconscious mind and from the subconscious mind to the Spirit or the Superconscious Mind. "That was not first which is Spiritual, but that which is natural (outward), and afterward that which is Spiritual" (inward). God accommodates His revelation to our realization or capacity to receive it.

Jesus explained our failure to receive the Spirit as due to our unbelief or our inability to recognize His Presence, and for this same reason the "natural man receiveth not the things of the Spirit of God, for they are foolishness unto him; neither can he know them, because they are spiritually discerned." Unless our subconscious minds are open to the Spirit they can only believe that which is outward.

Jesus said, "Know no man after the flesh" and "Call no man on earth your Father." Coming by way of manifestation is the way of disappointment and death. Our first knowledge of Christ, is after the outward form of Jesus, or the flesh, but He said, "Call me not good." Jesus was the personality of God, but it was only when the physical Jesus was taken away from the disciples that the Christ became an intimate and vivid reality to their souls. We must follow on until we have knowledge of Him in the Spirit, until we can say with the Apostle, "though we have known Christ after the flesh, yet now henceforth know we him no more."

Our knowledge of Christ, being revealed by the personality of Jesus, comes with observation; the second comes by realization and revelation of the Presence within us, without any objective manifestation. The first in order is the personality of Jesus, known in history. The second is a Divine revelation known only in consciousness. In the first we worship God. In the second we understand God.

By the mind of Christ we have "boldness to enter into the holiest by the blood (Spirit Life) or Jesus. By a new and living way, which He hath consecrated for us, through the veil, that is to say, His flesh." It is only within Christ consciousness that our desires find fulfillment on the manifest plane. It is only in Christ consciousness that we can know God. By staying the mind on Spirit we are fulfilling Paul's admonition to "let that mind be in you which was also in Christ Jesus." Not until we lose sight of the outward form are we ready to receive Spiritual revelation.

Jesus said to his disciples, "It is expedient for you that I go away, for if I go not away, the Holy Spirit will not come unto you; but if I depart I will send Him unto you." It is not until we cease to know Christ after the things of the world (using our power to get loaves and fishes) that we are ready to receive Him as the quickening Spirit. "It is the Spirit that quickeneth; the flesh profiteth nothing;" but "if I go . . . I will come again, and receive you into myself." He taketh away the first (personality), that He may establish the second" (Christ or Spirit). Let us not forget that "the way into the holiest of all was not yet made manifest."

The Mind of Spirit is the Mind of Christ. It is the clear consciousness which one experiences when he is absent from the body of related thinking. Spiritual consciousness is the consciousness of Spirit—of wholeness, completion and perfection. It is an enlarged edition of subconsciousness. It is the objective mind turned inward to the eternal consciousness which is God's expression of Himself.

Our conception of personality is all that stands between us and Spirit. Spiritual consciousness is latent in us all. It takes possession of us to the degree that we die to, renounce and lay down the personal consciousness and everything which it represents. "Leave all and follow me." We must do this until personality has no more power over us.

Resurrection is a new way of thinking and feeling. Spirit is a realization of all things, and of necessity will include a new consciousness of the body.

The requisite skill for living in Spiritual consciousness comes through practice. It can be acquired only as one constantly, consistently and persistently thinks, lives and acts according to the principles of Truth. Sporadic effort is worse than no effort at all. "We do not marvel at the instantaneous demonstrations of the accomplished athlete, musician or mathematician; but we are astonished and nonplussed because our Spiritual demonstrations demand an equivalent amount of preparation." Our imperfections and limitations have come to us as a result of our ignorance or misapplication of the principles of Truth. They can be corrected only by the understanding and proper application of these same principles. To think the Truth, live the Truth and act the Truth is to receive its reward. That which we seek is seeking us. It can come to us only as we make room for it in our minds.

Relying upon the promises of God, my imperfection is swallowed up in Perfection.

God Is Spirit

"And They Shall Not Teach . . . Saying, 'Know The Lord'!
For All Shall Know Me, From The Least To The Greatest."

Since God is Spirit—"The one and only Real Mind or Power in the Universe," and man is a mental or Spiritual being, he must related himself to God through his mental faculties. This is done by recognition and realization of the facts or Truth concerning God and man. "The heaven of heavens," said Solomon, "cannot contain Thee"—Principle.

It is impossible to conceive of such a vast idea of God until one's eyes have been annointed to see and one's mind has been opened to Spiritual understanding. When we are prepared to forget the things which are behind and reach forward to the things that are before, then will the Truth be revealed. "When the Spirit of Truth is come, He will guide you into all Truth;" "for the Spirit searcheth all things, yeah, the deep things of God."

To understand the deeper meaning of Divinity we shall have to use the word "Principle," which means simply a fact—(the fact of God). Principle then, is the basis of all our understanding about God and gives us the true or Spiritual interpretation of Him and His manifestation. When God said to Moses, "My Presence shall go with thee," He meant that man embodied the fact or principle within himself. It is obvious therefore that unless we approach God as Principle we have nothing to demonstrate and no rule of action. St. Paul refers to Principle as the "All-in-all," "Eternal," "Immortal," "the Only Wise."

"They that worship God must worship Him in Spirit and in Truth." The Principle must be spiritually discerned. That is, we must discover and apply it within our own minds, "for as the body without the Spirit is dead," so "the letter killeth, but the Spirit giveth life." The Principle is therefore the foundation upon which the Spiritual Temple (God consciousness) is to be built. "It is the porch that one must traverse to reach the altar. It is sown in mind a natural or literal word, it is raised up a supernatural or Spiritual Truth."

"Ye shall know the Truth." Principle is the allness of God and the Truth is that we are one with Him. We embody the God qualities within our own minds. We are inseparable as Principle and Idea. Principle is indivisible. It is perfect Unity. It is both cause and effect, — "The Self-Knowing Mind back of everything." It is that which knows us by what we know about ourselves. That in us which knows is Spirit or the Principle of Truth.

The I AM in man is the life of consciousness of man; "Without this 'I AM' man could not be." Thus, when we understand that the only consciousness we possess and which possesses us is God, we shall be able to demonstrate the Principle of Truth. It will proclaim Itself by means of our own consciousness through our recognition and realization of the facts concerning God and man.

Principle is Life and Life cannot be separated from living. Principle is consciousness and consciousness cannot be separated from mind. Mind is the only actor in the universe, therefore nothing moves except as Mind moves it. The qualification for the "greater things" which Jesus promised should be done in His name (Principle), as well as release from all unpleasant circumstances, was, to be so filled with the Spirit that there would be no room left for anything else. "The Spiritual or Christ consciousness only is substantial."

Jesus was a man like other men but conscious of His Spiritual Nature. He differed from other men in that He was one with God on the manifest plane. He recognized that His Christ was the Real Man of all men and identical with God. His awareness of the real Truth of His Being enabled Him to do all things.

"Open Thou mine eyes, that I may behold wondrous things out of Thy law."

The Five Activities of Spirit

Fundamental Law Is the "Path of Righteousness" (Ps. 23:3) – The "Way" – By Which the Soul of Man Is Restored to Its Original Perfection.

Life, Love, Mind, Spirit, and Truth are the five activities expressed in the one Life Principle. Life creates, Love attracts, Mind governs, Spirit expresses, and Truth sustains.

The basic meaning of these five aspects or activities of Principle is Permanence or Reality. "That which is permanent is real, that which is not permanent is not real." We would summarize then by saying that principle is the mental action and reaction of God upon Himself, and we find the purpose of Life stated in Jesus' words: "That they all may be one; as Thou Father, art in me and I in Thee, that they also may be one in us; even as we are one."

We shall henceforth think of God then, as the active Principle of good within our own minds – a Presence to be felt and a Power to be utilized. This correct view of God will give us power and dominion over our world. "As the Father hath Life in Himself, so hath He given to the son to have life in himself." God's Life is all life. God's Mind is all mind. God's Love is all love. God's Spirit is all spirit. God's Truth is all truth. God's Power is all power. God's Consciousness is all consciousness. God is both Creator and creation. He is the Conceiver and the conceived. The Thinker and the thought.

Understanding the Principle, we shall no longer make things by the uncertain and slow processes of the senses or human thought, but through the recognition and realization of the Presence of all good within ourselves. Living by our Principle, It will realize Itself in us without any effort on our part. We do not have to worry, struggle or exert the human will in any way. "In Thy Presence is fullness of joy." We find then the Truth of Jesus' statement that "things" are literally "added unto" those who seek His Kingdom first.

"The Lord is my shepherd; therefore, can I lack nothing." The "Lord" is the Law and the "shepherd" is our rule of action. The Law is impersonal and has no sentiment at all. It does not know how we use it nor for what purpose. The Law says to electricity, "Be a light," and it is a light. The Law says, "Run a street car," and it runs a street car. The Law is always obedient to our word. If a man says, "I am sick," the Law says, "I am sick." If he says, "I am poor," the Law says, "I am poor."

Just as the law of electricity does not know whether it electrocutes a little child or burns a house down, or whether it makes toast for our breakfast, so Principle does not know whether we are using it to make perfect or imperfect creations.

Principle is impersonal. The Law is a law of liberty which, because of the way we use it, becomes a law of bondage. But the bondage is never a thing of itself. It is simply the way we are using the law of liberty.

We are always dealing with the Law and by harmonizing the five activities of Spirit we are seeking to bring Spiritual values to bear upon the Law. In other words, we are using the Law constructively instead of destructively. The theory of Emergent Evolution is that, 'whenever our nature demands a new experience, there is that within this nature which projects the vehicle, making the experience possible."

Before we can use the Law constructively, there must be a complete change in our manner of thinking, feeling and acting. Remembering that "the mind of the flesh is . . . not subject to the Law of God," we must harmonize our mind with Divine Mind before there can be any increase of good in our lives.

"The Law of the Lord is perfect," and I will use it righteously.

The Activity of Principle

"All That the Human Soul Can Ever Need or Desire Is the Infinite Father-Mother Principle, the Great Reservoir of Unexpressed Good."

The Spirit of anything is the Principle of it. "All things were made by Him (Principle) and without Him (Principle) was not anything made that was made." Even to make the appearance of imperfection we have to use the Principle of Perfection. "In the beginning God" — Principle. "Closer is He than breathing, and nearer than hands and feet." The potentiality of one is the potentiality of all.

"All things are yours." Everything is equally within every man, but he must learn how to use his Principle constructively in order to draw it out. He must learn how to relate his subconscious mind to Spirit through which the Principle directly works. Metaphysics is not for the purpose of putting God into man, but to draw Him out of us. Unless God were already in us we should have no point of contact with Him.

When Jesus said, "I am the way, the Truth and the life; no man cometh unto the Father but by me," He was referring to the Principle of creation in all men. "The Way" is the "manner, method, mode; as, a way of expressing one's ideas. The means by which anything is reached or accomplished. Plan: habitual method of life or action, determined course." Man "cometh unto the Father" — Perfection, by the right application of Principle to his life.

"He that keepeth Israel neither slumbers nor sleeps." The Principle is always active in our minds, bringing us good or ill according to our association or relationship to It. The activity of every principle is creation. In music it creates notes. In mathematics it creates numbers. In metaphysics it brings man to a direct experience of God and that consciousness which produces all things. As "cause" it is imperceptible. As "effect" it is perceptible. The metaphysician assumes the position that there can be no manifestation of Perfection except in proportion as knowledge and the thing known, the subjective and the objective, are identified. We may say then, that Principle is the Universal Law of God which brings man and God together.

The Scriptural names for God are Life, Love, Mind, Spirit and Truth, and we classify the five under the name "Principle," which is the scientific rule by which we establish in consciousness what constitutes God. It is the means by which we come unto the Father, or gain our unity with Him. There is only one "way" to approach God. "No man cometh unto the Father but by me" — Divine Principle. The "me" is the scientific Principle which Jesus used and declared to all men. There is no other way to enter into Life, Peace, Harmony, Power and Plenty.

The difference between Jesus and other great teachers is that He was one with God on the manifest plane — "The Eternal manifested in the temporal," and that "He demonstrated His Spiritual or Eternal consciousness in the resurrection of the body, thus making the human trinity a divine unity.

The Principle of creation is inherent in all men and we shall discover God in our nature.

Our need and our supply are geared together. There is no adjustment to be made other than to keep ourselves relaxed in the mind of God. When all obstructing conditions have been removed the needed blessing will appear. It is comforting to know that God wants us to have what we want to have even more than we want to have it.

How then, you ask, does our good get to us? By a constructive use of Principle (initiating better causes) and by keeping open the mental channels through which the power of God can accomplish our desires.

> *"There is no power in conditions;*
> *There is no power in personality;*
> *There is only power in Thee my Principle."*

God's Idea of Himself

"Man as He Is, Is God's Idea of Himself. Man as He Appears, Is Man's Idea of Himself."

The Scriptures tell us that "God hath made man perfect" and that "All things were made by Him (Perfection): and without Him (Perfection) was not anything made that was made." It is quite obvious therefore that imperfection "was not made," — in other words, having no maker it has no existence. If God is the author of perfection which includes man, how could man be anything less than perfect? How could man created in God's own image and after His own likeness ever be anything but the manifestation of perfection? He could not and he never will.

How then did he come by the conditions of imperfection, disease, evil and death? If the true nature of man is Perfection why doesn't he express it now? Because is manifestation depends upon his evolution into the Christ or perfect consciousness. Man has talked a lot about perfection and thought a lot about it, but he has never realized it. Before we can know the Christ, we must be the Christ. Before we can express Perfection we must function in the consciousness of perfection or in that perfect state of mind which was also in Jesus. Before we can be the Christ we must discover the Christ within ourselves. "I and the Father are one." By our constant acknowledgment of One Presence and One Power we shall evolve into Spiritual or Christ consciousness.

Every man stands in the same relation to God as Jesus did. The difference between His works and ours is a quality of consciousness. He knew Himself as Christ, while we know ourselves as personality—"John Doe." Jesus believed in perfection and we see and believe in imperfection. "As I am, so I see." The power which He manifested was in His own consciousness, His knowledge of His own completeness.

When we know ourselves as God's idea of Himself, as Spirit and not personality, then we shall express our true nature, which is Perfection. God created perfection. Man created imperfection. God made the Spiritual world. Man made the material world. We are to bring the two together in consciousness by our understanding of unity, by the constant acknowledgment that all is Spirit. I am God (Spirit) and there is none else." "Hear, O Israel, the Lord thy God is One."

By knowing ourselves as God's Idea of Himself—we too can resurrect the body, heal the sick, and feed the multitudes.

The Presence of health is in the consciousness and not in the body. The Unity of Father and Son is the power that overcome the world.

The "Father" is that which is understood,—the **Recognition** of Its own perfection.

The "Son" is understanding,—the awareness and **Realization** of that Perfection.

The "Holy Spirit" is the Expresser,—activity of **Revelation** between the Father and the Son.

Thus the Truth is our power to know good an our power to unknown evil. "I and the Father are one."

If we let the numeral **(1)** represent good—that which is—and the numeral **(0)** represent evil—that which is not real, not made by God — we shall see that our constant recognition of the good **(1)** automatically dissolves the evil which is **(0)**.

To be self-conscious in God is to be conscious of Spiritual dominion. To be self-conscious in personality is to be conscious of material bondage. To keep the mind captive to the one (reality) will eventuate in self-completeness — Perfection.

"My perfection in Divine Mind is now established."

Metaphysics

"Divine Mind Is the Only Cause or Principle of Existence."

"Prove me now, saith the Lord," and "Be ye always abounding in the work of the Lord." The work of the Lord" or Law, is the correct understanding of God and the intelligent application of His Principle to all the problems and conditions in our lives. That which we know as "effects" in the relative world is simply the visible form and action of the Principle in manifestation. The Principle is ever active in our minds, operating in us according to our beliefs. "Prove me now" means the same thing as "Pray without ceasing." True prayer is the consciousness of one's unity with God. If the rule is applied we can never fail to get right results.

Jesus gave us the clue to Spiritual demonstration when He said, "I of mine own self can do nothing, but the Father, (Principle) He doeth the works." And again, "The Son can do nothing of himself." It is impossible for man to create anything, and the belief that he can is a sin against God. In the Divine scheme of creation, man's only office is to become aware of that which already is. When Isaiah said, "The government shall be upon His shoulder," he forever relieved man of any personal responsibility in demonstrating. The Truth known is instantly demonstrated or revealed.

To demonstrate the Principle or Law of God one must recognize as Jesus did that "The Father worketh hitherto and I work;" that he (individual mind) is but the means or instrument through which the Law of God operates. As man brings himself into a better alignment with the unchangeable

Principle, It will put him in touch with that Mind which "shall teach you all things and bring to your remembrance whatsoever I have said unto you."

The word "metaphysics" means literally "above things." Heaven, which is the ultimate goal of every seeker after Truth, is a perfect state of consciousness to which all things are added automatically, not by demonstration but by revelation. It is a state of completion in which one does not have to seek, pray, or treat, for any thing. "Christ is not the product of evolution," but the True Idea of the manifest world. As man by faithful repetition declares the Truth of that Idea, Heaven is revealed. As he holds the perfect Idea in mind, a perfect demonstration must automatically follow.

The one most important lesson we have to learn is that "The son can do nothing of himself," and that any personal interference or belief that we have anything to do is to delay the revelation. When we know that our mind is God's Mind, then our mind can only reveal that which is good. "Take no thought for the manifestation" if you have a perfect subjective realization. "That individual," says a great metaphysical writer, "is the best healer who asserts himself the least and thus becomes a transparency for the Divine Mind, Who is the only Physician: the Divine Mind is the scientific healer."

Health, happiness, peace, wealth, and power are established facts. They co-exist with the Christ. "And my God shall supply all your needs according to His riches in Christ Jesus." "All things exist in their essential nature as or in Spirit, hence the realization of Spirit (Christ) is equivalent to a realization of all things." As we acknowledge the Christ (True Idea) and cease to believe in error the Truth will automatically be revealed.

Jesus said, "Seek first the Kingdom (Principle) of Heaven and all these things shall be added unto you." They "shall be added" through our contemplation of the Christ. When the Principle is understood and applied there can no longer be any problem. Thus, to be properly related to Spirit is to be properly related to all things. As in mathematics, our only responsibility is to apply the Principle, Jesus said, "I knew these things were," and that is the first requisite in Spiritual demonstration—to know that what you seek has already been established. He used Divine Principle just as humans use the principle of mathematics. His unity with Spirit was so complete and His word so alive that He could instantly bring out substance, health, harmony and peace.

"One who wants the lights on does not stand and shout at the switch. He calmly touches it and thus closes the circuit so the power can come on. One who wants his roses to grow and bloom does not stand and scream at them. He quietly does the thing that provides them with Divine Supply, which does the rest. One who wants the Will of God done in his life or in the life of another does not need to tear his hair about." He only needs to "be absent from the body" (to open the channels) and God will do the work.

Our great blessings will come us when we have effected a perfect alliance with the Divine Will and they cannot come in any other way. The object of metaphysics therefore is not to change the Mind of God, but to change our own mind and to keep changing it until it conforms to His.

Relying absolutely upon Principle, I cannot make mistakes.

The Technique of Metaphysics

"Relax and Rest in the Consciousness that He Will Bring All Good to Pass in Divine Order."

"Trust in the Lord with all thine heart and lean not unto thine own understanding." Prov. 3:5.

The remedy for worry, anxiety, doubt, uncertainty, confusion and impatience is absolute trust in God. As we replace the worried, anxious thought with a thought of Trust we open the way for the free working of Divine Law in our lives. As we surrender the personal will for the Divine Will we discover that the power of God is greater than anything in the outer world. A man may believe in God but until he trusts his belief (gives himself to it) he cannot prove God. Until he trusts he cannot have dominion over the things of the world. The only time a man can be worried, fearful or anxious is when God is absent from his mind. It is impossible to worry and trust God at the same time.

Out of trust comes faith, out of faith comes conviction, out of conviction comes realization and out of realization comes revelation. These are the five steps by which we rise to absolute knowing and the assurance that "all things are yours." When we have arrived at Trust we have arrived at the place in consciousness where our word is converted into action. Trust, lifted to its highest level, is the word of God become flesh.

"God said . . . and it was to:

"Look unto me, and be ye saved, all the ends of the earth; for I am God and there is none else." It is not easy to trust that which we cannot see or to have faith in that which is imponderable and intangible. How can we look to that which is unseen? How can we trust that which is without form? Before we can answer these questions we must realize first of all that God is Spirit and not personality, and that His Principle must be Spiritually discerned.

To be absolutely scientific we must trust God in the same way that we trust the Principle of mathematics. "Acquaint now thyself with Him (Principle) and be at peace: thereby good shall come unto thee.:" By acquainting ourselves with the Principle of Life (thinking the Truth and filling our minds with thoughts of trust) our problems automatically disappear. Each time we trust God for the answer to some problem or for the favorable outcome of some desire, our faith is substantially strengthened. When we fail to get a right result it is not so much our faith is at fault, but our trust—a deeper realization that, "I can of mine own self do nothing." We need more use of the faith we have, it is true, but we cannot express more faith until we have more trust. "Faith without works is dead," and trust is the works of faith. It is that which puts our faith at work. It is the Power by which we become active in recognizing, realizing and revealing Truth.

The dictionary defines trust as reliance, assurance, and certitude. It is an attitude of mind toward God and the world in which there is no personal responsibility, no concern, no worry, no effort, and no fear. It is a settles state of feeling, and an utter reliance upon the fact that "all things are yours."

The great need in metaphysical practice is not performance but trust, confidence and communion. What we need is not so much the use of formulas but rather to establish that sense of unity between ourselves and God which makes intelligible conversation between Him and ourselves possible. The most effective results come through simple. The most effective results come through simple means. We must talk God's language if we expect good results from our work.

My mind is secure in trust, I give up all worried and anxious thoughts because I thrust God in all the affairs of my life.

"Have Received" — The Golden Key

*". . . Nor Height, Nor Depth, Nor Any Other Creature, Shall Be
Able to Separate Us From the Love of God."*

"Whatsoever things ye desire, when ye pray, believe that
ye have received them, and ye shall have them." Believing
that you "have received" is an open acknowledgement of
completeness or ease. Believing that you have not received
is an open acknowledgement of incompleteness or dis-ease.
According to Jesus, the Kingdom called Heaven is a state of
ease or satisfaction, while the place called earth is a state of disease or separation. "In the world ye shall have tribulation." To
be a little more specific, these two states considered from the
standpoint of mind represent the two poles of consciousness;
i.e., God consciousness and self consciousness.

Wishes, wants and desires are for the most part in the realm
of things, designated by Jesus as "loaves and fishes." The
represent certain values and limitations of the human mind.
But the literal meaning of "Seek ye first the Kingdom of God"
is the attainment of that condition of consciousness which
would be designated as "having received" everything that
you had wished for. This is not a beautiful platitude, but an
exact, scientific statement of Divine Law.

Could that Kingdom be lacking in anything? Then what
would it mean to have the Kingdom within oneself? It would
mean a realization of completeness or wholeness which would
necessarily include every wish or desire. Since it is impossible
to realize completeness and incompleteness at the same time,
an acknowledgment of Heaven (completeness) would leave

nothing to be desired, thus fulfilling Jesus' promise that "all these things shall be added unto you." They shall be added in our realization of completeness or "having received."

There is a fine point here which most students fail to perceive, namely, that one cannot be conscious of desire and completion, of having received and not having received, at the same time. The things we desire are in our thought and what is in thought is least of incompletion in the conscious mind which produces separation, dissatisfaction and dis-ease.

"Take no thought," said Jesus, for it is the only way in which one may get away from the condition of consciousness which is the basis of his desire. Our conclusion therefore is, that no one may expect to be well or whole whose mind is occupied with unfulfilled wishes, wants or desires. Until these are eliminated (made of no importance), we cannot enter Heaven (wholeness). The moment we take thought about things we are in bondage to them, and by the very nature of Principle, which is continuity, must continue to lack them. "Acknowledge Him in all thy ways and He will give thee the desires of thine heart," but, again, the acknowledgement of the Presence (wholeness) comes first.

The Truth is, that until one can forget or obliterate every "thing" from his mind he cannot contemplate or realize the all-ness or completeness of Heaven.

As stated elsewhere in this book, Heaven must come to us through a new state of consciousness. To St. Paul the Lord said: "My grace (self-sufficiency) is sufficient for thee: for my strength is made perfect in weakness." This means that our greatest good comes to us when we are taking no thought about it. Weakness in this sense refers to the detachment of the conscious mind. The degree of detachment determines the manifestation of our good. When human thought (attachment) is weak, God becomes strong. When we let go of desire we break the continuity or bondage which is the basis of our lack. Satisfaction, completeness and wholeness are States of Being expressing themselves in a consciousness of "having received."

Jesus said, "These things have I spoken unto you . . . that your joy might be full:" but joy, again, is not a state of having any particular thing, but a State of Being. The greatest joy that could come to any man would be to be wholly conscious of God's Presence, which would be equivalent to having everything that he desired.

The most effective prayer is the clearest realization that we already have that which we seek. We got the clear realization that in Spirit we have that which we desire and we behold it coming into visualization but the open acknowledgement of completion. We can see at once that this is a prayer of both understanding and faith. When in praying you get the realization that what you desire is already yours you may be sure that answer to your prayer will soon appear in manifestation. You may be sure that you have entered that high consciousness in which prayer and answer are one.

"Satisfaction, full, complete,
Fills me with its fragrance sweet;
Health of body and of mind
In the living Christ I find."

The Truth

"One cannot embody Divine Perfection as long as he entertains a finite or personal conception of himself." — God's Workshop.

Self-consciousness pursues God.
Christ consciousness possesses Him.
Personality approaches Principle.
Christ is always at the point of spiritual understanding.

"If ye shall declare anything in My Name (consciousness) it shall come to pass." It was Jesus' mission to give man an understanding of life which he could apply to every detail of his living. "I have declared Thy name unto them and will continue to declare it." It is "in His Name," that we prove God and lay hold of His promises. It is in His Name that "The former things have passed away; they shall not be remembered nor come into mind any more," — the former things being all the diseased and imperfect beliefs and limitations of the human mind.

To declare a thing is to make it known. Before we can learn the Truth of anything we must embody the facts concerning it. We must test them by our understanding. Just as we learned the multiplication table by our faithful repetition and declaration of the facts concerning it, so we learn the Truth of God by declaring and embodying those things which we know to be true. Before we can have that mind in us which was also in Christ Jesus we must declare and embody the Truths which He taught. The rule is stated in the words: "If ye abide in me and my words abide in you, then ask whatsoever ye will . . . and it shall be done unto you."

Realization of the Truth is the activity by which we abide in Him and keep His words, and by which we have His mind in us. To have His mind in us is to be united in consciousness. Just as the principle of mathematics solves problems in arithmetic or the principle of music brings out harmony, so the Principle of God brings out His substance and perfection in our lives. When Jesus said, "Ye shall know that Truth, and the Truth shall make you free," He meant that true thinking would produce true or spiritual results. There is a vast difference between knowing the Truth and talking the Truth. It is the difference between revelation and demonstration. Jesus said "Know the Truth," and the Truth (Spirit) does the work. Truth is established. WE do not have to demonstrate It, but to recognize, accept and realize that It IS. The demonstration has already been made and all we have to do is to become aware that It is—not will be.

Truth is the True thought of man about the world and God. "Christ in you" is the Truth of you—the Spiritual Savior of the world.

THE TRUTH

1. There is only one Presence and one Power in the Universe, which is all good and all powerful.
2. God is all there is and beside Him there is none else.
3. Man is a Spiritual being embodying the Life, Mind, Spirit, Truth, Love, Intelligence, and Law of God. He is living in a Spiritual world. now.
4. Man's body is Spiritual and perfect now. The substance of man's body is pure spirit.
5. The mind of man is an Infinite possibility embodying the omnipresence, omnipotence and omniscience of God's Mind.

6. All things in the relative world are related to man's mind as ideas and are under the domination of God's Mind.

7. Heaven is a mental state of harmony which can be experienced now.

8. The Christ is man's point of contact with God—his power to know the Truth and to apply Spiritual law.

9. The will of God is the best that man can conceive for himself or another.

10. The word of God is the beginning of all creation.

"Christ in you, he hope of glory."

Ye Shall Know the Truth

"When He, the Spirit of Truth, is come, he will guide you into all Truth."

Many of the commandments of Jesus are paradoxical to those who read them with the fleshly mind. The very words which present Life to the Spiritually illumined. only seem to set forth contradictions to those who read them in the light of human understanding. To Spiritual consciousness they are "a savour of life unto Life." To the human mind they are "a savour of death unto death." It is only in one's detachment or absence from the body that the Truth is revealed. At one time Jesus said, "Ye shall know the Truth and the Truth shall make you free." At another He said, "Take no thought." How is one to know the Truth if he cannot think? The answer is, that as long as a man thinks he knows something he cannot know God; he is in bondage to the thing he think he knows.

God is self-knowingness. For God to know himself in us would be Truth. For us to know ourselves in God would not be Truth. "The natural man receiveth not the things of God, for they are foolishness unto him." Thus, if the human mind thinks it knows something it must continue to experience that thing. If it only thinks or reasons about Truth it is not in a condition to know it. The continuity of human thought can be broken only as one leaves all theories, human opinions, and instructions, in fact "the entire knowledge of this world," and enters into a deep realization of the Presence of Spirit. "Leave all and follow me."

God is not a glorified consciousness of things, but a glorified consciousness of Himself. Since it is in the natural mind that we find all sin, sickness, laws, bondage and error, one must leave that mind in order to find Truth. Not until we come to the end of our confidence in ability to do things can God do anything for us. "The son can do nothing." "Not that we are sufficient to think anything as of ourselves; but our sufficiency is of God." And St. Paul said. "'If a man thinks he is something when he is nothing only deceives himself." It is true therefore that we cannot be "free" as long as we are in bondage to an opinion or a belief.

The Truth is man's power to be aware of that which is true. But human knowledge is not true. The knowledge of health as Truth, for instance, does not save one from the knowledge of sickness as error. In the natural mind both health and sickness are within the realm of human knowledge, but they have no place whatever in the Christ mind. Trying to rid oneself of sickness as error by denial, merely sets up a battlefield in consciousness, for both are beliefs which show the power of the mind to think or know anything it chooses; the Knower is always greater than that which is known. It is by virtue of what we are that the Truth is revealed and not by virtue what we think.

Knowing the Truth is like the reflection in a mirror. If we think of mind as a mirror reflecting intelligence and Truth as man's power to recognize the reflection, we shall see that knowing the Truth about ourselves involves no strain or effort whatever. The Truth, just as the image in the mirror, reveals Itself. Hence Jesus' statement, "Take no thought." Why does man look into a mirror? To see himself. Why must one know the Truth? To discover his Spiritual identity. Stillness reveals

73

the Truth to him. When Jesus said, "Know the Truth" He meant simply that we need a greater realization of that which is already known. To realize what we already know is to be "free."

All evil and and imperfection springs out of the action of man's mind upon himself, which action is referred to in the Bible as the devil, Satan, and evil spirit. Jesus called this use of the mind "a liar which standeth not in Truth because there is no truth in him."

To be consciously one with God therefore one must lose his fictitious self and follow the Truth. He must separate himself from the consciousness which is untrue and identify himself with the real and perfect.

"Turn ye unto with all your heart."

Applying the Truth

"The Truth can have nothing outside Itself, other than Itself, nor unlike Itself, by which to divide Itself. Truth is indivisible."

It is not the study or application of Truth which is hard, but trying to understand man's conceptions of It. When the mind is open toward God the Truth is simple to understand and apply. Intellectual knowledge of Truth does not satisfy the Soul. St. James said, "Be ye doers . . . not hearers only." It is only the Truth which we apply that makes us free and now is the time to begin.

"NOW is the accepted time," for everything.
NOW is the time to have faith in God. . . . Omnipresence.
NOW is the time to trust God.
"NOW is the time to be kindly affectioned one toward another."
NOW is the time to be loving.
NOW is the time to be harmonious.
NOW is the time to be peaceful.
NOW is the time to be unselfish.
NOW is the time to enter Heaven.
NOW is the time to be true.

As we think the true thought about anything we are applying the Truth. As we speak Heavenly Words we are practicing the Truth. Heavenly Words are whole words. They are those which have no association with, or relationship to, anything on the manifest plane—Peace, Joy, Happiness, Love, etc.

Man's Consciousness is his power of response. He is constantly responding to either good or evil. Every experience calls forth some kind of a response from us. By our words "we shall be justified and by our words we shall be condemned." "A man's words (thoughts) are his only burden." If we respond to an evil experience with thoughts of criticism, condemnation, worry, or fear, we are hiding the Truth. If we respond to the same experience with thoughts of peace, blessings, harmony and praise, we are revealing the Truth. By watching every experience and making the right response to it, we are knowing the Truth about it—we are renewing the mind.

The Christ Mind sees through deception. The human mind intensifies it. Human consciousness believes in something to be healed. Spiritual consciousness disbelieves in disease. Jesus said, "How can one enter a strong man's house (consciousness), and spoil his goods, except he first bind the strong man?" We are bound by our own freedom. Mind is responsive intelligence. Man thinks and his mind responds to his thought. If man responds to a negative experience with a negative thought he brings forth a false creation. If responds to the same experience with a positive or true thought he brings forth a true creation. Truth cannot free us from our problems until we change our attitude toward them.

St. Paul said, ". . . overcome evil with good." Since both evil and good are in our minds, we neutralize the evil by magnifying and giving power to the good. The mind that says, "I am sick, I am weak, I am poor," is the same mind that says, "I am well, I am strong, I am rich." In the latter case man is bearing witness to the Truth. In the former he was bearing witness to evil. We overcome the evil by affirming or making know good.

"God hath not given us the Spirit of fear; but of power and of love and of a sound mind." Let us watch, lest, having given a problem over to God, we do not take it back again by our conscious thought, fear or worry. We must be fearless, steadfast and thankful. "Judge not according to appearances." If a problem should again appear after you have turned it over to God, do not doubt nor fear, but simply give thanks that it is in His hands, that He is taking care of it. When knowing the Truth about a problem, you must cooperate with God by letting Him do the work through you.

You must cooperate with him by refusing to have anything more to do with the problem.

"Beloved, NOW are we the Sons of God."

Two Classifications of Consciousness

"Man has two natures. He must identify himself with one."

If man's soul and body are to be healed of their present imperfections, he must develop a new kind of intelligence and a new order of consciousness. He must have something more than beautiful thoughts, words, theories, affirmations and denials. He must use something more than his will and intellect. Thinking is automatic. It proceeds from a certain state or quality of consciousness and must reproduce that state regardless of what the thinker says to the contrary. As longs as a man is under the law of his own thinking, he is as he thinks, and not what he thinks he is.

The "hid treasure" is the Christ consciousness, referred to also as God consciousness, and the Kingdom of Heaven. It is that changeless state of perfection which knows no opposite and nothing unlike Itself. Jesus gave us the scientific rule for developing this new order of consciousness when he said, "Seek ye first the Kingdom of God and His righteousness and all these things shall be added unto you."

Are you seeking healing? Are you seeking money? Are you seeking the things of the world? If you are, the you are not applying the rule. Thousands of students make the mistake of seeking things first. They do not understand that the Kingdom consciousness is the unvarying Principle of all things or completeness, and until they have that sense of wholeness, they seek things, Jesus said, "Ye seek me for the loaves and fishes and ye cannot find me." In the new order of consciousness (wholeness) "My God shall supply all your need." "Your heavenly Father knoweth what things ye have need of." "Before they call I will answer."

Actually there are but two classifications of consciousness, which are the material (self) consciousness and the Spiritual (Christ) consciousness. The first has to do with life on the manifest or earth plane and includes body, personality, human beliefs and all the hard and set rules of the human mind. The second has to do with life of the Spiritual plane and with "My Father's business;" with knowledge of God, and with Christ and Spiritual Law. As consciousness functions on this latter plane, it sets aside and invalidates all that seemed true on the material plane. "If ye be in Christ (Spiritual consciousness) ye are above the law (of the material) and not subject to it." As we "leave all" on the lower plane, new ideas, new capacities, and new abilities will be revealed to us. As we follow Him, a new order of health will take possession of us.

The scriptural words for consciousness are "soul" and "heart." "Keep thy heart with all diligence." "Out of the heart are issues of life." "Out of the abundance of the heart the mouth speaketh," etc., etc. We must protect the soul from the invasion of the outside world by changing our habits of response. "Judge not according to appearances but judge righteous judgment.

Now, what is the predominating character of your consciousness? Is it material or is it Spiritual? Every man must determine this for himself. Do you draw your life from the outer world through the senses, or do you live by the inspiration of the consciousness of the Presence within you? In time of great need does your thought turn automatically and naturally to God or to personality? What is the character of your thought, feeling and action? Examine all your attitudes toward life in the same way and the decide upon a definite course of action. "Be ye transformed by the renewing of your mind." Our consciousness must be made all over again by an inward response toward God. We have the power to do this. We have the power to make ourselves think what we want to think. We have the power to reject every idea, thought or suggestion which does not conform to the Christ standard of perfection.

On Which Plane Do You Work?

"For One Is Your Master, Even Christ."

There is something pathetically strange about Jesus' words. "Behold, I stand at the door and know," and especially so when we consider how frequently and ignorantly we have used His power to make imperfect and discordant conditions of consciousness. Life is infinitely pure and perfect, but being impersonal and passive, It suffers man to use It as he will. He can use it to work out conditions of sickness, limitations and death, or he can use It to work out the true Idea of his Spiritual self.

There is little a man can do about his heredity until he adopts a new Father, or pattern for his thinking. Jesus said, "Whosoever he be of you that forsaketh not all that he hath, he cannot be my disciple." If we would make a new and perfect consciousness of ourselves. If we have been using the Principle of Life ignorantly to make imperfect conditions, we must now use It Intelligently to make perfect conditions.

Conversion is not a change of mind, but a change of relationship. When we open our doors to the Christ we simply ally ourselves with the Truth of our being and make it dominant in our lives. As we adopt a new Father we inherit perfection instead of imperfection, health instead of disease, wealth instead of poverty, and peace instead of confusion. The best way to destroy the negatives in our lives is to cultivate the positives. The best way to destroy imperfection is to cultivate perfection. When Jesus said, "Behold, I stand at the door and knock," He meant that He was offering to us the Christ as a substitution for all the evil in our lives. When the Christ Idea is introduced, the evil and imperfect conditions wither away. The personality loses its power as we cultivate the Christ.

Is there any health in a diseased body? There must be or we would not feel sick. Since God — the good — is everywhere present then there is always latent within any imperfection, the Principle of Life or Perfection. "Call upon me (Christ Consciousness) in the day of trouble; I will deliver thee." The perfect Idea is the leaven hidden in the three measures of meal. "Our remedy is always at hand, nearer than any doctor or medicine." God is Responsive Intelligence — as we call upon the good the lower nature loses its power. It is obvious therefore that a man's body cannot be healed until his consciousness of the body has been healed. The Christ cannot appear until the personality has been changed.

On which plane do you work? If you make your metaphysical statements on the objective plane you are only denying what you know to be a fact. Every thing is just as real as it is believed to be. In the body consciousness disease is a fact and no denial of the fact is going to change it.

Truth statements are important if there is anything in us that says they are not true. Jesus said, "I and the Father are one," but no one can know his unity with God in the objective mind. It is in Spiritual consciousness that Truth statements are true. "To the pure all things are pure." In Christ consciousness we are able to heal not by virtue of what we say, but by virtue of what we are. When we contemplate ourselves and others as Spirit in an everlasting NOW it will be impossible to fit disease concepts into that which eternally is. We must not say what we do not believe.

Disease is sequential, known only to the objective mind. In Christ consciousness there is no sequence and no disease. If we declare the Truth in Spiritual consciousness it is true and has the power to change the manifestation. If we declare the Truth in objective consciousness it is not true and has no power to change anything. That which is Real is permanent: that which is unreal is impermanent. The objective body is changeable and therefore healable, when we are one with the true idea.

"It is no longer I that live, but Christ liveth in me."

The Problem of Mind

He Builded Better Than He Knew;
The Conscious Stone to Beauty Grew.

— Emerson.

"Plato likens man's mind to a charioteer driving two horses, one black and fractious, ever pulling downward, the other white winged, striving heavenward; and it takes a skillful driver to keep such a team pulling together." Until man's consciousness and subconscious minds are synchronized — made to pull together — his word is powerless to change the evil effects in his life. "He that wavereth is like a wave of the sea, driven by the wind and tossed. Let not that man think that he shall receive anything from the Lord."

There is no limitation upon the demonstration that any man can make, but the outcome of his prayer depends upon his subjective embodiment, or realization, of the word he speaks. The answer will always be proportionate to the soul's acquiescence to the statement of the lips.

The solution to every problem is contained in the problem. The answer comes out of the problem; God is in man. Life is in man. Therefore is a Principle and we must cooperate with It in the way It works. The Principle does not put God into man, but helps him to express that which is already there. One does not go to a music teacher to have music put into him, but have it drawn out.

Jesus said, "According to your faith be it done unto you." God will give to us as much as we can consciously receive, but we can only receive as much as our mental equivalent or belief allows. The one using the Principle must become embodiment of it. When a prayer is answered it is because the man is praying has moved himself into a right relationship with Principle and because his subjective mind accepts what his objective mind decrees. When Faith touches Spirit, the Principle responds.

The whole purpose of prayer is to cause the subjective mind to believe. The prayer does not change God, but the mind of the one praying. If the conscious mind believes and the subconscious mind denies, it is a house (consciousness) divided against itself. There must be both recognition and realization before there can be a revelation.

God is the Gift, the Giver, and the Receiver. We do not have to ask God to be God. "God is God," Life is Life, and Truth is Truth.

Jesus said, "As you believe (know the Truth), it shall be done unto you." The Principle does to each one of us and gives to each one of us — not as we think, but as we believe and know. To correlate the two-fold mind, then, we must have both belief and the embodiment of the belief. When there is no longer anything in us which denies our word then the two minds may be said to be working in perfect harmony.

At first the subconscious mind is very much like an unruly child. It must be taught to obey. It must understand that you mean what you say. It must be so convinced of your statement that contradiction is no longer possible. Having no reasoning power of its own, "the subconscious mind is even more credulous than a child." It is dependent at all times upon your directions and commands. If you are firm and steadfast in your position (yourself convinced) and give your subconscious mind a proper patter or idea from which to work, it will heal the body, solve problems and work out any ideas to be developed.

There is, of course but one mind, but like the body it has various functions. All mind is one mind and yet it is the use of mind that determines what a man's life is to be. The function of the conscious or objective mind is to choose what it will have. The function of the subconscious mind is to accept the idea and give form. If it does not accept the idea then the prayer is not answered. It becomes "clouds without rain." If the man who makes the prayer wavers, the subconscious mind will waver also.

Jesus said, "Ye ask and receive not because ye ask amiss." Most of our prayers, treatments and declarations are made in the upper mind, which explains why the results of our work are so pathetically small. Failing to touch Reality, they do not come to birth. "out of the heart are the issues of life," and unless our prayers gets down into the soul (subjective mind) it is impossible for God to act upon it, our soul is being the connecting link between the conscious or Divine Mind. The first works voluntarily; the second automatically. "Thou shalt also decree a thing and it shall be established unto thee."

Finally, the fundamental need in practice is to have the consciousness or capacity to receive. We should pray less for things and more for an ability to be receptive to the blessings of God. As we increase our state of awareness, we increase our capacity to be more receptive to the health, substance, Life and power of God.

Say many times a day with deep feeling and in perfect faith: I know that my subconscious mind receives my word and acts upon it.

Clearing the Mind

"Casting Down Imaginations and Every High Thing that Exalteth Itself Against the Knowledge of God, and Bringing Into Captivity Every Thought to the Obedience of Christ."

"For the things which are seen are temporal; but the things that are not seen are eternal." To work on the divine basis one must put Spirit first; "In the beginning God." The command to "put first things first" is generally disregarded by the mind that seeks only "loaves and fishes." It tries to save it's life and have it too. It tries to heal the body while believing it is sick. Judging from appearances, it knows only what it is happening in the outer world. It tries to do works of Jesus Christ without possessing the consciousness for which they stand.

"Leave all" tears away from man everything that he formerly knew as himself, everything in the body of thought which knows both good and evil. As longs as the consciousness of evil remains, evil must be expressed, whether it is injustice, disease, poverty or death. Until the world of appearance has been completely dissolved man is not ready to step into the new dimension (consciousness) of Jesus Christ, which is unconditioned, unlimited and unrelated. How can we see man as perfect if we are seeing him as the same as sick, sinful or dying.

"In My Father's House are many mansions," (states of consciousness). Jesus said nothing about preserving the old personality and body which is no longer a fit instrument for the soul: "Loose it and let it go," He said, and "seek those things which are above." Enter into a new state of consciousness where all things automatically become new. "This is (present tense) Life eternal, to know Me." To know "Me" is to have the capacity to do all things which were impossible before. "Whereas, before I was blind, now I see."

If we examine carefully the States of Being in a previous study we shall see that every one of them is above the realm of consciousness which no association with anything in the world of effects. Every one of them is a Spiritual fact or state of Divine Being eternally available and accessible to every man. As we dwell in them from day to day they will gradually form in us a consciousness and body which they represent. We shall remake our consciousness of the world. We say glibly that God is Spirit, but it is a known fact that God cannot be Spirit to us until our conception of the world is spiritual. In other words, we cannot know God as Spirit as long as we are knowing or feeling an opposite which is designated as matter. Either God is Spirit or He is matter. He cannot be both.

There is much work to be done in clearing the subconscious mind of tis false beliefs, preconceived ideas and imperfect judgments but "He taketh away the first that He may establish the second." "He must increase, but I must decrease."

"There is no peace until the old errors are turned out, and the soul is emptied of its belief in the experience of the senses." "Blessed are the pure in heart for the shall see God." "To the pure all things are pure." out of purity comes peace. Out of peace comes poise. Out of poise comes power. Out of power comes plenty and out of plenty comes perfection. "Be ye therefore perfect even as your Father in heaven is perfect." The States of Being are not states of having something we did not formerly posses. They are states of Boing. "If two (consciousness and subconscious minds) shall agree touching any point, it (perfect correlation between the two) shall be established on the earth." Perfect agreement with Spirit is to have everything supplied at the right time.

"That which ought to be is; therefore let us rest."

Educating the Mind

Spirit Is the Great Educator Which Quickens Man's Mind to Receive and Accept as His Own the Divine Attributes – Modes of Being.

The Most effectual way to break up sub-Spiritual states of consciousness is to first determine what we will recognize as Reality or Truth. We must have a standard (the highest possible), and abide by it in all our dealings with the world.

Remembering that conditions are crystalized by habitual mental states and feelings, we must train ourselves to thing affirmatively and positively.

Healing does not depend upon what God may or may not do for us, but upon our ability to cooperate with the law that is already in operation. Adjustments must be made from our own position in relation to that which is perpetually good and perfect.

We must first deny all the material conceptions by separating them from the believer.

We must supplant the old beliefs with new and better ones.

We must admit only those concepts which are True or in harmony with Christ.

Our choice is between Christ and chaos, between peace and conflict, between Divine Order and confusion. We are punished by our ignorance and not for our sins. As we gradually deny and break down the old ways of thinking and feeling they will atrophy from want of use. As we bring the mind under its Spiritual dominion the senses will cease to bring evil into our lives. When we are sure that we are divine instead of human then our world will be a much better place to live in.

We must stop pouring metaphysical platitudes into the shallow depths of our objective minds and address ourselves to the more serious and important business of evoking (drawing out) the realities that are already lying dormant and inactive within us.

The word education is from the Latin e-ducio which means to lead out, not to pour in. The education that results in complete living is the only one worthy of our consideration. To "acknowledge God in all our ways" is to come into a consciousness of a new state of Being. Regeneration begins when we are rightly related to those qualities of mind which represents God or the Christ Self in us.

THE CONSCIOUS TUNING OUT OF THE NEGATIVE BELIEFS

The ideal of Spiritual unfoldment is to have such a deep consciousness of the Presence of God that there is no longer any response to negative suggestions. We must develop a new way of thinking, feeling and seeing. We already have all the faculties by which to realize the Spirit objectively, but we must use them toward the end. If we objectively believe that "God is all," then we must stay our minds upon the fact until our consciousness becomes all good.

"God hath made man perfect." Within the Mind of God is a perfect Idea of every man, but man must work out God's Idea for himself. He must work It out by a process of elimination. Before the Divine Self becomes the Supreme Self in man he must destroy all the beliefs which cause suffering in his life. He must enter into the various States of Being until he is possessed by them.

The secret of increasing the knowledge of Spirit within us is stated in Meister Eckhart's words: "If the soul were stripped of all her sheaths, God would be discovered all naked to her view and would give Himself to her withholding nothing. As longs as the soul has now thrown off all her veils, however thin, she is unable to see God."

I am receptive and obedient to the Mind that is seeking to lead me into my Perfection; I offer no resistance.

Formulas for Re-Educating the Subconscious Mind

We Work Out Our Salvation by Establishing Ourselves in the Reality of Being

Heaven is the place of immediate demonstration.

Did you ever stop to consider what it would mean to have a consciousness which took no account of evil, to have your thoughts demonstrated instantly, to have the answer to a problem before it appeared, to be able to speak a word and have it fulfill itself without any effort of your part? These are but a few of the natural consequences of one's ability to think clearly in the Mind of God.

Jesus said, "Seek first the Kingdom of Heaven." What is Heaven? Heaven is an enormous extension of Life, health, peace, power and plenty. How do we "seek the Kingdom"? By Turning all our energies and faculties toward Principle and by increasing our awareness of the Spirit within us. "Thou wilt keep him in perfect peace whose mind is stayed on Thee." Peace, therefore, is the necessary condition by which one enters into a direct experience of God.

> "Truth is within ourselves; it takes no rise
> From outward things, whate'er you may believe.
> There is an inmost center in us all,
> Where Truth abides in fulness; and around
> Wall upon wall, the gross flesh hems it in, . . . and to
> know

Rather consists in opening out a way
Whence the imprisoned splendour may escape,
Than in effecting entry for a light
Supposed to be without."

The whole object of these formulas is to enable man to become in outer manifestation what he is is in Spirit, and to cause the soul to identify itself with the Truth of its Being instead of its personal characteristics. The work necessarily must be done in Spiritual meditations by slowing down the action of the objective mind. Each one of these statements should be directed to the soul and should be persisted in until it realizes itself in us without any effort on our part.

We do not concern ourselves with the senses in this work nor with the faculties of the human mind, but only with the Christ within us. It is advisable to take each one of the states of Being and abide in it until there is a definite unity in our conception of the words or until our understanding of them is Spiritual or "without variance." This may take weeks or months or even years, but the senses having failed, we must be willing to "pay the uttermost farthing" for Reality.

FORMULAS

Speaking to the Soul:

1. You, my real self are Spirit. In you there is no matter.
2. You, my real self are Power. In you there is no weakness.
3. You, my real self are health. In you there is no sickness.
4. You, my real self are ease. In you there is no dis-ease.
5. You, my real self are wealth. You are my freedom from poverty.

6. You, my real self are Life. In you there is no death.
7. You, my real self are knowledge. In you there is no ignorance.
8. You, my real self are Faith. In you there is no fear.
9. You, my real self are Unity. In you there is no strife.
10. You, my real self are Love. In you there is no hate.
11. You, my real self are Truth. In you there is no error.
12. You, my real self are Peace. In you there is no trouble.
13. You, my real self are God. In you there is no personality.
14. You, my real self are righteousness. In you there is no wrong.

I can accomplish any ambition of my soul provided I make every other purpose subservient to that ambition.

Correlating the Mind

In Unity, There is Strength.

Jesus said, "No man cometh unto the Father, but by me," — Christ, — the perfect state of mind wherein the individual soul or subconscious mind is perfectly integrated with the Mind and Will of God. Transcendental philosophy defines this correlated state of mind as power To know, To be, and To do.

When Paul said, "let Christ be formed in you," he meant that we are to make the mind sensitive to good by quickening our responsive to Spirit. "Be ye transformed by the renewing of the mind." The one thing that vitally concerns us in Spiritual work is to change the subconscious habits of beliefs, and the more we quicken our response to Spiritual impulses the less conflict and opposition there will be to the word of which we speak.

"Blessed are the pure in heart for they shall see God." As we gradually dispossess our subconscious partner of its evil and false beliefs by magnifying the good and refusing to believe in appearances, it will be take up into God. "If any man will come after me let him himself." "He that loseth his life shall find it." If we are really serious about putting on the new man which is Christ we shall have to deny the consciousness which now makes up our life. We shall have to renounce the feeling and knowledge of ourselves as flesh and think of ourselves as Jesus thought of Himself — "Before Abraham was I Am."

The four-fold plan of salvation is

Renunciation which is a denial of the self according to appearance. "Call no man on earth your Father."

Recognition—seeing ourselves as we are in Spirit and in Truth.

Realization—feeling the Truth of ourselves as of one substance with the Father.

Revelation—which is the absolute knowledge of Spirit, Soul and Body as a divine Unity. Then, "we shall see Him as He is."

Since it is a law of mind that it assimilates that which it believes and reject that which it denies, the body will always express the quality or nature of the soul. If the soul is material, the body will be material. If the souls is Spiritual the body will be Spiritual. Thus, to experience a new condition in the body we must have the consciousness which the Divine Idea represents. When the two minds pull together (cooperate in complete harmony) then the individual is at the point of dominion and authority. He can speak his word with absolute confidence and it will accomplish that whereunto it is sent.

The difference between answered and unanswered prayer is the difference between a unified and a divided mind. The wavering man is the one who does not know what he knows nor believe what he says. When we truly believe in a thing it must come to pass. When the mind is perfectly integrated with our word, then it becomes flesh and dwells among us. Faith is complete only when thought and feeling vibrate in perfect harmony, only when there is no longer anything in the subconscious mind to oppose our word.

The method of correlating the two minds is as follows:

1. Relax all mental tension in the mind,—animosities, fears, jealousies, hatreds, injustices, and negative beliefs.

2. Forgive and forget all the contradiction, disturbances, and resentments by replacing them with their opposite qualities.

3. Convince your subjective mind that you mean what you say.

4. Be persistent. We are transformed not by our occasional thought but by our prevailing and habitual states of mind.

5. Be patient. It has taken years to build your imperfect conditions and you must change them a little at a time. "In patience ye shall win and possess your soul."

6. Be absolutely ruthless to all divided states of mind. Repeat a hundred times a day if necessary: —"Thou shalt worship the Lord thy God, and Him only shalt thou serve."

7. Magnify the good. Look for the good in everybody and everything. Tell your subconscious mind that it can receive only the good.

8. While in meditation repeat the following statements until the subconscious mind is perfectly synchronized with the conscious mind:
   a. I am one with my own divine self.
   b. Not my personal will, but Thy Divine Will be done in me.

If we are persistent in this work our mental attitude will be transformed. The secret of power is to be in unity with Divine mind.

"Today I will comply with the voice of my clear-thinking Self and not be overruled by habit."

What Is Faith?

"Well Done Thou Good and Faithful Servant: Thou Hast Been Faithful Over a Few Things, I Will Make Thee Ruler Over Many."

"Faith is the substance of things hoped for, the evidence of things not seen." Fait is God! Faith is Substance! Faith is Life! Faith is Truth! Faith is Health! Faith is Confidence! Faith is Assurance! Faith is Freedom! Faith is Realization! There is nothing but Faith—faith in good, faith in evil.

Faith is man's power to act upon the Substance, Mind, Spirit, Life, and Perfection of God. Faith is man's power to heal every disease and to educate himself out of every imperfect belief.

Imperfect and evil condition are kept alive by our faith in them. They sustained by the power of our faith and the repetition of them in our minds. There is nothing but faith, and without faith man's world comes to an end.

Belief is passive. Fait is active. Being impersonal and positive, faith acts upon everything with which man identifies himself. We can cultivate belief, but faith was give to us. It grows with the exercise of our trust. A man can believe whatever he wishes to believe, but it is by faith that he enters into his beliefs and keeps them alive.

Since faith is always positive and always active it is the power that increases good or evil in our lives No matter how we may use it, faith works. Being a combination of thought in negative states of consciousness as it does in positive states.

Fait is impersonal. Fear, for instance, is faith in evil. It is faith turned the wrong way around.

But faith in appearances is just a strong as faith in God. Faith cannot change from itself. When man disbelieves in sickness, poverty and discord, faith must then work for his health, wealth and harmony. We can change the manifestations in the outer world only changing our beliefs in the mind.

The reason for so much sickness and poverty in the world today is because man is content to remain in personality. He is always trying to make his faith in personality do the works which belongs to Spirit. He trusts personality and looks to it for his good. Jesus said, "The arm of flesh will fail you," and we read of Him that, "He did not commit Himself unto them, for he knew what was in man." The ever recurring disappointments of misplaced faith will attend the man who trusts personality for his good. Mas has all the faith in the world. What he needs is more faith in good, which will produce more good in his life.

If an ignorant or wrong use of faith has brought evil conditions in our lives, we should see them as stepping stones to a more positive and God-like use of our faith. "The depth of our valley can then be the height of our mountain." We can turn evil conditions into good ones by changing the identity of our beliefs. Our fears will prove to be blessings if we can see them as our capacities for faith. Personality says, "Of mine own self I can do nothing." Faith says, "God can do all things through me." When man's faith is perfectly integrated with the will of God then nothing is impossible to him.

According to St. Paul, faith is both the substance and evidence of things not seen. Faith does not materialize substance but allows us to be physically conscious of that which eternally is. It is our consciousness of a thing that makes it real to us. It is our consciousness that clothes it with physical identity. Our faith then is our consciousness; or the essence of the thing itself. Thus God as faith within us is both the substance and evidence of everything needful in our lives.

Out of the substance of my active faith, my hoped-for revelations are formed.

Putting Our Faith to Work

"Have Faith In God"

We learned in our previous lesson that faith is the power of our own minds to "Hold fast that which is good," or to hold fast that which is evil. It is the sum total of all our human experience. Faith works the way we use it. Belief is experimental. "Faith is positive action." Belief is impatient. Fait is patient. Belief seeks signs. Faith is its own evidence. Faith is the realization and proof of things not seen. IF things have not been going well with us then we need to change the object of our faith. What we need is not more faith, but more faith in God. We need to exercise our faith in the right way.

When the faith of man is perfectly integrated with the faith and will of God then man has limitless power to accomplish anything he wishes to do. God says, "I will never leave thee nor forsake thee." Thus, when we do our part God will not fail to do His. Faith is the most faithful thing in all the world and we must claim it now. Since our capacity to receive from God is always measured by the capacity of our faith, we need to enlarge those beliefs until they can recognize the All-Presence of God.

We have the promise that "all things are yours." Then why ask for things? Could an Infinite God think in terms of things or look to the world of His good? IF we inwardly knew that "all power is give unto us in Heaven and earth," would not our word have the power to find its form in

103

the visible? Would not this very consciousness have the power to speak the world Health and put to an end the conditions of sickness, or the word Perfection and bring forth a manifestation of wholeness to replace the conditions of imperfection?

Faith is an attitude of mind against which there is no longer any contradiction possible to the mind that entertains it. If that mental attitude is identified with God then that is faith in God. IF that attitude is identified with one's ability to do any particular thing, then it is his ability to do that thing. Knowledge in itself is insufficient, for unless we act upon the knowledge we have, we shall get no results.

He who trusts God speaks with authority. He who only believes in God speaks with uncertainty. Trust is the activity between knowledge and faith. When we trust God absolutely He does the work for us. To trust God therefore, would be to recognize as Jesus did, that "It is done." When there is no longer anything left in the subjective state of our thought to contradict the statement of our lips, the the work is done. The most difficult thing we have to do is to neutralize those beliefs which contradict the reality of the word which we speak. We can do that by saying many times a day, "I have faith in God, not man." "I have faith in health, not sickness," I have faith in wealth, not poverty." "I have faith in strength, not weakness." "I have faith in good, not evil." "I have faith in unity, not separation." God is Omniscience—all Knowledge, (the answer to every problem.) God is Omnipresence—all Presence (knowing only Itself). God is Omnipotence—all Power (the activity of Spirit in all our affairs.) God is here. The answer is here. The substance of everything we need is here. Have faith in God—the Good.

Absolute faith in One Presence and One Power relaxes the mind so that the substance and power of God may flow through us without hindrance. The important factor is realization is faith. As we keep the mind open toward Principle the power of God can accomplish our desires.

Since "Belief is purely intellectual," and "Faith is properly Spiritual," I surrender my changing beliefs to a substantial faith.

Prayer

*Our Faith Comes in Moments . . . Yet There is a Depth in
Those Brief Moments Which Constrains Us to Ascribe More
Reality to Them Than to All Other. — Emerson.*

"What things soever ye desire, when ye pray, believe (be
firm) that ye receive (present tense) them, and ye shall have
them." This is the exact law of prayer: — Believe and you shall
receive; doubt and you shall not receive.

The object of prayer is not to gain God's attention but to let Him
hold ours. The law of mathematics will not solve a problem
in arithmetic or algebra any more than the law of electricity
will light a house or run a street car. "Laws of themselves are
helpless to do or undo anything for us." Man must use the
law for definite purpose and specific needs. He must set the
law in motion and specialize it through his own mind.

The Kingdom of Heaven is finished, and the only purpose of
prayer is to help us to see It as It is. We shall always perceive and
experience as much of Heaven (wholeness) as our individual
consciousness permits. Heaven is our consciousness of IT,
but so is our sickness, so are your problems and our miseries.
Jesus' method of prayer was to make agreement with His
good. Recognition must always precede realization. Unless
prayers take us into a new consciousness of our unity with
good, they become clouds without rain."

"Agree with thine adversary quickly, whiles thou art in the
way with him." The adversary here referred to is the collective

name for everything which separates us from God. The first step in scientific prayer therefore is to agree, or forgive all the evil and limitation in our minds. "The son of man hath power on earth to forgive sins." Until we can make the evil unimportant, we cannot affirm the perfection which we know to be real.

The word "forgive," as stated elsewhere in this book, means literally to absolve or pardon the evil and the replace it with the good. It is ridiculous to believe that God forgives sin when, as Habakkuk tells us, He knows nothing about sin. Since man is the only sinner and the maker of all evil in his life, he himself is the only one who can forgive sins and evil or make them of no-importance by his agreement with Divine Law. It is because Lazarus was alive that Jesus called him from the tomb. It was because there was an abundance of food that He fed the five thousand. It was because the idea of man's arm was perfect and changeless, that Jesus commanded him to stretch forth. It was because there are no blind eyes or dear ears in Spirit that Jesus could by His spoken words open them. "And God saw everything that He had made, and behold it was very good."

Before the miracle of turning water into wine Jesus said, "Fill the water-pots with water." To the fishermen He said, "cast the net on the right side of the boat." To the grieving widow he said "Weep not." Before feeding the five thousand he commanded the people to sit down. And in order to get water, the three kings were told to make the valley full of ditches. Prayer, to be effective, must be affirmative and positive. There must be a perfect union between the mind and will of man and the mind and will of God. God helps them who help themselves.

He gives to those who "believe" or relate themselves to that which they want. Prayer is not true until there is an absolute recognition and acceptance of that which is about to appear. Filling the pots with water and casting the net on the right side of the boat were symbolical of the acknowledgment or belief in the gift. "The reason Jesus was to become the Christ, was that at the objective point of his thought there was complete realization of the unity of the Spirit and the absoluteness of His word."

"I turn to God in love and faith, for he hears my innermost prayer."

Rules of Prayer

". . . Grant That Through Me Thou Shalt Show Them
How To Pray Aright."

1. "Prayer is the science of inducing (in mind) concepts, acceptances and realizations of peace, poise, power, plenty, health, happiness and success, or whatever the particular need may be."
2. We must harmonize our will with God's will. "Let the will of God be done in me."
3. To receive an answer to our prayer we must have the consciousness for which it stands. The act of man is followed by the act of God.
4. "Pray without ceasing." The very best prayer in the world is a continuous effort to think straight.
5. "Listen greatly to yourself." Every prayer begins and ends with your thought. It is an action and reaction of the mind upon itself. Every man answers his own prayer through his belief or mental equivalent.
6. We are to ask in the "name" or nature of Jesus Christ, — (in Spiritual consciousness.)
   To ask "in His name" is to recognize our own sonship, divinity and perfection, become ourselves the embodiment of the God powers as manifested in Jesus Christ.
7. "Before they call, I will answer:" The Kingdom of Heaven is finished. "It is done." All we need to do is to see It as It is.
8. "Desire is not something to be worked for, but it is the thing in its incipiency pressing towards us for expression."

9. The real nature of prayer is set forth in Jesus' statement, "Consider the lilies how they grow. They toil not: neither do they spin."

10. "Ye shall decree a thing and it shall come to pass." It shall come to pass when you recognize that God's work is done and you are merely relating yourself to it.

11. When we pray we must not become anxious about results. "in quietness and confidence shall be your strength."

12. "Before Abraham was, I AM." God is working for you all the time. Know, therefore, that He is already doing the thing that you are asking Him to do.

13. Pray first for a whole mind, and all other desires will be fulfilled automatically.

14. Instant answers to prayer come through man's unity with God—when man and God are in perfect agreement.

15. "All that I have is thine." Convince your subjective mind that it is not only God's will, but His desire, to give you everything you can ask for and take.

16. "I know that Thou hearest me always." To be on speaking and receiving terms with God, we must be one with His Consciousness, which is the perfect relationship between Father and Son.

17. "I thank Thee, Father, that Thou hearest me." Prayer should begin and close with praise and thanksgiving. The prayer of praise and thanksgiving opens the mind to receive.

18. "Pray to thy Father which is in secret." To pray in secret is to close the consciousness to the outer world. Just remember that God cannot answer our prayer if we are thinking of things. We are not truly in The Presence if we are feeling lack or limitation of any kind.

19. "And thy Father which seeth in secret shall reward thee openly." When our consciousness of God overbalances everything else, the prayer is sure to be answered.

20. "I have a way ye know not of." God will find a way even where there is no way.

21. The secret of answered prayer is contained in the following words: "If ye abide in me, and my words abide in you, ye shall ask what ye will, and it shall be done unto you." To abide in Christ is to have immediate access to God. To live in the Spiritual consciousness is to share His Life, His Power, and His Substance.

22. "Therefore I say unto you, all things whatsoever ye pray and ask for, believe that ye have received them and ye shall have them." The difference between conscious and actual possession of a thing is the knowledge that we "have received" it. The world of things will always respond to the conscious state of "have received."

23. "God does not bring to birth and not bring forth." If our prayer is not answered, it is because we have only affirmed. "Ask — Believing." To complete the circuit there must be both affirmation and realization.

24. Make an end of prayer. "Now, when Solomon had made an end of praying, the fire came down from Heaven and consumed the burnt offering and the sacrifices; and the glory of the Lord filled the house." God steps in when man steps out. To make an end to the prayer we must leave it in God's hands and take no more thought about it.

Through prayer, "Thy highest thought for me" shall be fulfilled.

The Great Universal Solvent

"For the Peace of Heaven, Now Manifesting As Harmony in My World, God of Peace, I Am Thankful."

"Acquaint now thyself with Him, and be at peace: thereby good shall come unto thee." Infinite and eternal peace has been defined as that quality of consciousness which would be induced through contemplation of the statement, "The earth is without form and is void;" i.e., fulfilling St. Paul's behest to "be absent from the body and present with the Lord."

The greatest experience of God is peace—"the peace that passeth all understanding." It is the power by which we enter the Kingdom of Heaven and the power by which we remain there. "Thou wit keep him in perfect peace whose mind is stayed on thee." When we have completely detached ourselves from the realm of things (ourselves included) that which remains is peace. "My peace I give unto you." No other gift is so great, for peace is that condition of consciousness through which God directly works. It is that element in which all our prayers are answered, and through which all our good comes to us. "Seek peace and pursue it, thereby good shall come unto thee."

In the truest sense, metaphysics is an abstract science and until one gets on the Spiritual basis (above things) its principles simply do not work. To illustrate this point we shall call attention to the fact that if you were going to write an important letter you would not think of writing it on stationery that had already been used. You would instead take a perfectly clean, new piece of paper. In metaphysical science our work must be done in Spiritual or "clear consciousness." We must have a new state of consciousness before we can express new effects.

"Put off the old man and put on the new," which is Christ. "The new which is Christ" is that mental state wherein the world is "without form and void." Now, since all our problems, difficulties, diseases and discords are in the world of personality and things, and since it is impossible to be conscious of Infinite Peace and trouble at the same time, one needs only to enter the abstract quality of Peace to get away from the disturbing elements in his life.

Infinite peace is an unvarying, changeless state of Being which knows no possibility of reaction to discord or any change from Itself.

Peace is not the lack of confusion or noise. The Truth is, that confusion and noise are the lack of peace. We enter peace in such degree as we become peaceful, and the secret of enduring peace is to keep our minds "stayed" upon the power and goodness of the present moment.

The greatest enemy to peace is the wasteful habit of allowing the mind to think ahead and to dwell upon future uncertainties. Every time we go over problems or anticipate solutions in our minds we are only increasing the problem and dividing the energy which will be needed when we come to it. When the mind and affairs are in turmoil we need only to identify ourselves with Infinite peace to get immediately away from them. Hold your peace and remain free, for when the soul has entered into a deep realization of God's wonderful peace, the things of the outer world will no longer have power to disturb you.

The mind that is stayed upon the power of peace will attract only peaceful conditions to itself.

*This day I am free from all worry and anxiety because
I put my whole trust in God.
The peace of God now fills my heart, and extends to the very
circumference of my world.*

Raisa - Mystic Alchemist

Energy Healing, Chakra Alignment, Sacred Geometry, Sound Healing

Tammy:

I was blessed with a healing session by Raisa last week. She felt like a friend and like-minded gentle soul with comforting Mother Mary essence pouring through her words. Raisa was so in-tuned to my blocks and traumas held within my field. She used her connection to ascended masters I've resonated with such as Yeshua, Mother Mary, Mary Magdalene, Lady Vesta & Amethyst and archangels Metatron, Michael and others to help clear these.

I was able to address childhood trauma situations to flip the stuck energy I've held onto over the years. She also picked up on a few traumatic past-life scenes that have affected my current life. I am an intuitive energy healer who truly felt the shift and healing within. I now feel so much lighter and have clarity regarding my path.

So much love and gratitude to you both, Raisa and Barry for presenting her to my world! (More Testimonials on following Pages)

Contact Raisa to book an Energy Healing
or Chakra Alignment session:
www.RaisinYourIsness.com
raisinyourisness@hotmail.com

Shannon:

This BEAUTIFUL sister...our Raisa... is a treasure beyond compare! After my experience in my personal session with Raisa... the ABSOLUTE confirmation I received, that could ONLY be confirmed by HER mind you... this session solidified EVERYTHING for me. I KNOW that this sister... she is a formidable, magnificent & IRREPLACEABLE component in this Earth plane story we all are invested in! IF YOU ARE DRAWN TO HER FOLLOW YOUR HEART

No other can do what SHE is gifted to do for YOU... YES YOU!

I LOVE YOU dear sister! I am forever grateful for what only you could do and DID for me! I would have happily paid any price for what you gave me! I URGE YOU ALL to schedule a session with this beloved one!

P.S. thank you Barry for sharing her with us all!

∞

Natasha:

I would like to thank Barry for introducing us to Raisa. I have had 2 consultations with her in the last month and I am in total awe of what transpired. Raisa is such a beautiful caring soul! She connected with me as though she has known me forever. Her love and dedication in assisting others is so touching. I had an amazing experience and some profound healing. I received a message from Jeshua which brought tears to my eyes. I could feel the LOVE in the message that was given to me and I will remember and cherish His message forever. Raisa has really helped me in confronting fears, trauma and past life karma. I have found the reason for my skin problems which I never would have thought it'd be possible. It is amazing what guilt and shame from past lives can actually do to your body. Her healing and that from our Angelic beings has really made a huge difference in my life. I can feel it in my energy. Raisa has a lovely sense of humour, always reminding you not to take life and yourself so seriously. I really feel like a heavy weight has been lifted off my soul. Thank you so much! Much Love!

∞

Ariel:

Raisa... Divine Raisa... You are a Treasure to this Life, and I thank All That Is, and this also Treasured YT channel for the priceless blessing which was our session this AM. Every moment of the session was a fractal explosion of wonderful intuitive & divinely guided perfection. I honor your sincere, caring, graceful, playful, soothing, encouraging, transformational, empowering, and so beautiful demonstration / embodiment of Goddess energy and presence. I am so honored & thankful to have been guided to You. To have invested in the patience, time, energy, and resources to share sacred healing and uplifting time with You. I will remember the session Always. And I will look forward to any and all ways our Creator deems it harmonious to connect again. I could go on and on and on, so please accept my parting acknowledgment of your blessing to this realm, my Heart & Spirt, my Life, and the Lives of all those who may be positively impacted via your assistance. Blessings, and Gratitude, a thousand times over and over again. Namaste... Namaste... Namaste...

∞

B.G.

I have just finished a healing session with Raisa. The experience was remarkable! I am still buzzing! I heard about her from this channel, so thank you deeply Barry!

Raisa is so lovely to talk to, and intuitively guided, knows how to get to the hidden roots of our issues. She calls upon ascended masters, archangels and such to do deep energetic clearing and healing work. It was like being guided through the deep layers of myself, releasing the things that don't serve me and filling every cell with light. I purged, and I absorbed new energy, and came out feeling uplifted and renewed. Raisa helped me to find things in myself that I had been cut off from, and to heal wounds I had tried to bury. She has also given me helpful ideas to continue to improve things my life.

I am so blessed to have found Raisa, and ever grateful for the healing work she has done. She is as authentic as they come. Truly an earth angel! Thank you, thank you, thank you!

▶ YouTube